COMPUTING
MADE
EASY
FOR THE OVER 50s
WINDOWS 7 EDITION

Which? Books are commissioned and published by Which? Ltd,
2 Marylebone Road, London NW1 4DF
Email: books@which.co.uk

British Library Cataloguing in Publication Data
A catalogue record for this book is available from the British Library

ISBN 978 1 84490 112 8

1 3 5 7 9 10 8 6 4 2

The publishers would like to thank Sarah Kidner, Matt Bath and the Which? Computing team for their help in the preparation of this book.

Consultant editor: Terrie Chilvers
Project manager: Emma Callery
Designer: Blanche Williams, Harper-Williams
Proofreader: Chris Turner
Indexer: Christine Bernstein
Printed and bound by Charterhouse, Hatfield
Distributed by Littlehampton Book Services Ltd, Faraday Close, Durrington, Worthing, West Sussex BN13 3RB

Essential Velvet is an elemental chlorine-free paper produced at Condat in Périgord, France using timber from sustainably managed forests. The mill is ISO14001 and EMAS certified.

For a full list of Which? Books, please call 01903 828557, access our website at www.which.co.uk, or write to Littlehampton Book Services.

COMPUTING
MADE
EASY
FOR THE OVER 50s
WINDOWS 7 EDITION

Contents

COMMUNICATING

PHOTOS, VIDEOS & MUSIC

MAINTAINING YOUR PC

SECURITY

TROUBLESHOOTING

RESOURCES

INTRODUCTION

Using a computer needn't be a stressful experience. With this book you can get to grips with your Windows 7 PC and find out how to get the most out of it. From basic tasks such as how to save a document to fun activities like sharing your photos or listening to music, you'll find step-by-step instructions and advice that's easy to understand.

Computing Made Easy is designed to guide you through everything you need to know to become a competent computer user. Once you've found your way around your computer in the early chapters and mastered the basics, you can move on to other topics such as using the internet, emailing or chatting online via a webcam. Later chapters will show you how to manage your photos, music and video footage, as well as how to keep your computer secure and in good working order, plus lots more.

You can either work through the book chapter by chapter, dip into a specific chapter, or use the Contents page or Index if you want to find advice on a particular subject.

There's no time like the present – turn on your computer and let's get started.

EDITORIAL NOTE

The instructions in this guide refer to the Windows 7 operating system. Where other software or websites are mentioned, instructions refer to the latest versions (at the time of going to print). If you have a different version, the steps may vary slightly.

Screenshots are used for illustrative purposes only.

Windows 7 is an American product. All spellings on the screenshots and on the buttons and boxes in the text are therefore spelled in US English. The rest of the text remains in UK English.

All technical words in the book are either discussed in jargon busters within the text and/or can be found in the Jargon Buster section on page 213.

GETTING STARTED

By reading this chapter you will get to grips with:

 Finding your way around your PC

 Using the keyboard and mouse

 Understanding Windows

▶ The Basics

GET TO KNOW YOUR PC

Whether you've just bought a new PC or want to get to know your current one better, here's a list of important features to look out for.

DISC DRIVES
Desktop PCs come with a CD/DVD drive. The most common drives let you both play discs and record (burn) CDs and DVDs (a DVD-RW drive). Desktop PCs are also available with drives that can read Blu-ray discs, which can store a lot of data, including high-definition films. Blu-ray disc writers are also available, but are expensive.

MEMORY
Your computer's short-term memory, or RAM, determines how many programs can run simultaneously. Depending on what you'll be using it for (video-editing, for example, uses more memory than word processing software), 2GB RAM is suitable for an average user.

MONITOR
Modern PCs will come with a flat-panel LCD (liquid crystal display) monitor, whereas older PCs may have a much bulkier CRT monitor.

SPEAKERS
Your computer will already have a soundcard, but you'll need speakers to hear the sound.

PROCESSOR
Also known as the central processing unit (CPU), this is the engine of your computer and determines its speed (measured in GHz/gigahertz). A multi-core processor has more than one CPU on a single silicon chip, so it's better at handling multiple tasks at the same time. For a basic machine you'll ideally need a dual-core processor running at about 2.5GHz.

OPERATING SYSTEM
The software that runs your computer. PCs now usually come with Windows 7 (see page 14). Older computers may have Windows Vista, Windows XP, or earlier as their operating system.

HARD DISK DRIVE
Where your computer stores all your software and files. Until recently, hard drives were measured in gigabytes (GB), but now it's not unusual to see terabyte (TB) hard drives. Most desktop PCs come with 300GB or more, which should be plenty – but bear in mind what you'll be using your computer for. If you're storing a lot of photos, videos and music, you can quickly use up your hard disk space. If in doubt, always go for more space.

GRAPHICS CARD
Responsible for displaying images on your computer. An integrated graphics card shares your computer's RAM (memory), which often makes the computer slower. If you plan to play games, edit videos or watch films, you will need a dedicated graphics card, which has its own RAM, and will perform well without drawing on your computer's memory.

MOUSE
Used to move your cursor around the screen. There are two main types: ball and optical. Optical mice operate by emitting a light from an LED or laser, while ball mice rely on a mechanical system of rollers and an internal ball. A mouse can be wireless or connected with a USB or firewire cable (see page 12).

POWER SUPPLY
Plug your PC's power supply cable in here. Your computer may also have an on/off switch at the back (although you will rarely need to use this). To turn your PC on, use the button at the front.

ETHERNET PORT
Sometimes called the network port, this lets you connect computers over a network or plug in a modem or router.

FIREWIRE PORTS
Firewire cables transfer data to and from digital devices, such as digital camcorders and MP3 players.

MONITOR SOCKET
This is the where you plug in your monitor cable.

USB PORTS
Many devices, such as printers and scanners, connect via USB ports. You may also have a USB port on the side of your monitor.

KEYBOARD AND MOUSE PORTS
These are often colour-coded, or will have an icon next to them. Newer devices may connect via USB.

SPEAKERS AND HEADPHONES
Sockets where you can plug in sound devices. They're often colour-coded with icons to help you plug into the right one.

TIP
You can add extra storage to your existing PC by investing in an external hard drive (see pages 188–9).

NEXT STEP

Once you've set up your computer, you'll want to get online (see page 68).

▶ The Basics

YOUR DESKTOP EXPLAINED

The desktop is the screen you see as soon as your start up Windows.
Here, you'll find icons linking to documents, programs or specific
areas of your computer.

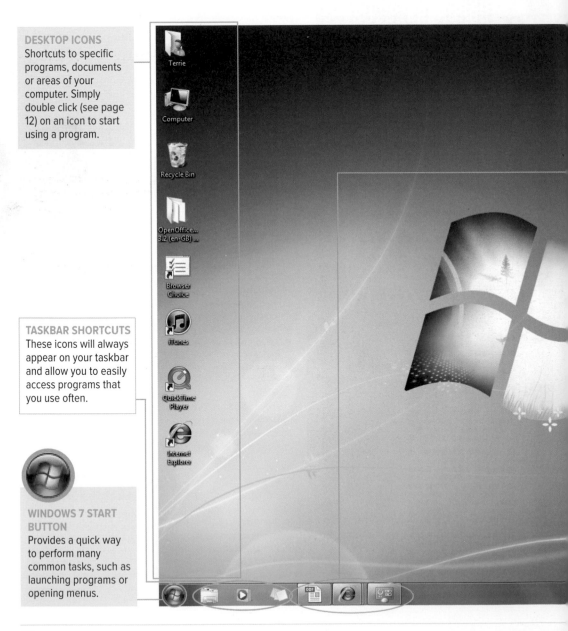

DESKTOP ICONS
Shortcuts to specific
programs, documents
or areas of your
computer. Simply
double click (see page
12) on an icon to start
using a program.

TASKBAR SHORTCUTS
These icons will always
appear on your taskbar
and allow you to easily
access programs that
you use often.

**WINDOWS 7 START
BUTTON**
Provides a quick way
to perform many
common tasks, such as
launching programs or
opening menus.

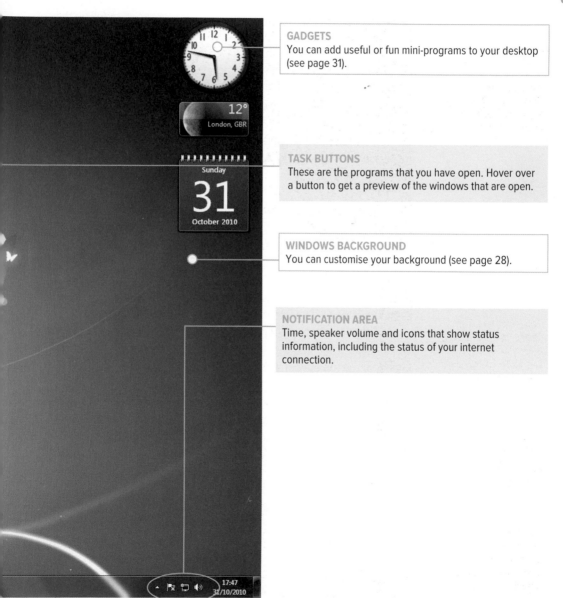

GADGETS
You can add useful or fun mini-programs to your desktop (see page 31).

TASK BUTTONS
These are the programs that you have open. Hover over a button to get a preview of the windows that are open.

WINDOWS BACKGROUND
You can customise your background (see page 28).

NOTIFICATION AREA
Time, speaker volume and icons that show status information, including the status of your internet connection.

THE MOUSE

The majority of computer mice feature two buttons and a scroll wheel. Here's how to get to grips with your mouse.

If you buy a new mouse, you usually won't need to uninstall the old one. Simply unplug it, plug the new one in and it should work straight away. However, some mice come with special software that will allow you to take advantage of advanced features, and you will need to follow the manufacturer's guidelines on how to add this software.

Single click Sometimes referred to as left-clicking, this involves clicking the left-hand mouse button just once. Whenever you're instructed simply to click on something, this means a single left click.

Double click Clicking the left-hand mouse button twice in quick succession is known as double-clicking. You often need to double click on an icon to open a program, or on a document name to open a file.

Right click Pressing the right-hand button, or right-clicking, often reveals a list of functions you can perform. Highlighting text (see below) and right-clicking within a Word document, for example, reveals options to change the appearance of a paragraph.

Highlighting Click your mouse at the beginning of the paragraph and keep it held down. Drag your mouse cursor to the end of the paragraph or section of text and release the mouse button. Your selected text will be highlighted and you can right click to access further actions (or use the toolbar at the top of your screen).

Drag and drop Mostly used to move objects or documents from one place to another. For example, to move a file from one folder to another, click once with your left-hand mouse button to select the object, keep the button depressed and drag towards its new folder. The file will move with the cursor; let go of the mouse button to drop the file into its new location.

Scrolling Most mice have a scroll wheel between the left- and right-hand mouse buttons. To scroll down, click on the page once and roll the scroll wheel towards you. Alternatively, press down on the scroll wheel and roll the wheel towards or away from you to move down or up a page. If your mouse doesn't have a scroll wheel, click on the up or down arrow on the right-hand side of any page, or drag the bar if it's a long document or web page.

TRY THIS

Often hovering your cursor over something will reveal another menu without the need to click on anything at all.

THE KEYBOARD

SHIFT KEY
You can use the shift key to type a capital letter, by pressing it at the same time as a letter key. Press it with other keys and you will get an alternative symbol – for example, combined with the '1' key, you will get an exclamation mark.

FUNCTION KEYS
Perform specific tasks depending on which program you're using. For example, pressing F5 in Microsoft Word will bring up a box that allows you to search for a specific word in your document. Pressing F5 when you're using the internet will reload (refresh) the web page you're looking at.

CTRL KEY
This key is used in combination with others to perform certain functions (see below for some examples).

THE WINDOWS KEY
Pressing this key will open up the main Windows 7 menu.

ENTER
Also known as the return key. You can often use this key once you've submitted information (on an online form, for example) and want to progress to the next step. It will also start a new line on a Word document.

Selecting files Click on a single file to select it. If you want to select a number of files at once – for example, to delete multiple files or attach various documents to an email – press and hold the **Shift** key and click on the top and bottom files in the list to select all the files in the list. Alternatively, you can select miscellaneous files (every other file, say). Hold down the **Ctrl** key and click with your mouse on every file that you wish to select.

Copy and paste To copy a section of text or an image, highlight the relevant text or image, then press **Ctrl** and hold while you also press **C**. Then move the cursor to the location you want to copy it to, press **Ctrl** and hold while pressing **V**. This is useful if you want to copy information on a web page, for example, into a Word document or email. If you want to cut text completely from one document and paste in another, highlight the relevant text, then press **Ctrl** and hold while pressing **X**. Then paste as above. Pressing **Ctrl** and **Z** will undo the last task you performed (for example, if you delete a whole paragraph by mistake and want to get it back).

NAVIGATION KEYS
Allow you to move around in documents or web pages. Most do what they say. Pressing the Home key will take you to the start of a line if you're using word processing software; the End key will take you to the end of a line. Pressing the Insert key forces any text you type to overwrite what's already there (rather than insert it).

▶ The Basics

UPGRADING TO WINDOWS 7

Most new PCs come with Windows 7 pre-installed. There are three versions
– Home Premium, Professional and Ultimate. Windows 7 Home Premium is
usually the best choice for a home user. If you have an existing computer,
you can buy a boxed copy of Windows 7 from a computer retailer.

Depending on which operating system you're currently using, you will
need either a full or upgrade-only version.

Upgrading from Windows Vista

It's more likely that you'll be able to opt for an upgrade installation, but
this very much depends on which version of Vista you have. By and large,
if you're going a 'like-for-like' route, you shouldn't have a problem.

If you have Vista Home Basic or Home Premium, for example, you will
be able to choose the upgrade installation if you're moving to Windows
7 Home Premium (or Windows 7 Ultimate), but will need to run a clean
installation (see page 16) if you're switching to the more advanced
Professional or Enterprise editions. For more details check here:
www.microsoft.com/Windows/windows-7/get/upgrade-considerations.aspx.

Upgrading from Windows XP

If you're currently using XP, you'll need to check that your computer
meets the minimum system requirements of Windows 7. These are:

- ▶ 1GHz or faster 32-bit or 64-bit processor
- ▶ 1GB RAM (for 32-bit) or 2GB RAM (64-bit)
- ▶ 16GB free hard disk space (32-bit) or 20GB (64-bit)
- ▶ DirectX 9 graphics card

To find out how to check your computer's specifications, go to page 209.
Alternatively, you can use the Windows 7 Upgrade Advisor (see opposite).

Providing your XP computer meets the minimum specifications for
Windows 7, you can upgrade to Windows 7 by performing a clean/custom
installation (see page 16–17). Similarly, a clean installation is required for
anyone wishing to add Windows 7 to a computer running anything other
than XP or Vista. So if your PC has Linux installed or if it's a bare bones
system with no current operating system software at all, you'll need to
buy a full edition of Windows 7 and perform a clean install.

WINDOWS 7 UPGRADE ADVISOR

The Windows 7 Upgrade Advisor will assess the suitability of your computer and the compatibility of the software and hardware.

1 Type www.microsoft.com/windows/windows-7/get/upgrade-advisor. aspx into the address box of your web browser and press **Enter**

2 Click on **Download the Windows 7 Upgrade Advisor**

3 On the next screen click **Download** and then **Save**. Save the file on your desktop

4 Locate the file on your desktop – it should be called Windows7UpgradeAdvisor.msi – and double click it

5 Click **Run.** On the next screen, click **Next** and read the license terms. If you're happy with them, tick **Accept the Licence Terms**, then click **Next**

6 Click **Install** (if you're using Vista, a User Account Control warning may appear – click **Continue**)

7 Click **Close** to finish

Starting to use the Upgrade Advisor

1 You should now find a new shortcut on your desktop – double click this to start the Advisor (again, if you're using Vista, a User Account Control warning may appear – click **Continue**)

2 Make sure all of your equipment (e.g. printers, cameras) is plugged in and switched on then click the **Start check** button to run the Advisor

3 Scroll through the results to see if there are any compatibility issues listed – green ticks are good, yellow exclamation marks denote something that may require attention, red crosses indicate a possible incompatibility

4 The Advisor will suggest an action to take in each case

the basics

INSTALLING WINDOWS 7

Buying Windows 7 on its own means installing it in one of two ways. An upgrade install layers the new operating system over the top of your old one, theoretically preserving all your files and programs. A clean install (see below) involves wiping all the existing data from your computer's hard disk and then installing a fresh copy of Windows 7 (see opposite). A clean install requires backing up your personal files first, and restoring them manually once the process is complete. You'll also need to reinstall programs, such as Microsoft Office, from the original disc.

If you are upgrading from Windows Vista, you can use the upgrade option. However, if you are upgrading from Windows XP, you will need to do a clean install (as long as your computer meets the requirements for Windows 7 – see page 14). You are now ready to perform a clean installation of Windows 7.

✓ **Upgrade options available**

Starting the installation

1 All editions of Windows 7 are available as either a full or upgrade version. As long as your PC is running a licensed copy of Vista or XP you can perform a clean install with either so it will be fine to buy the cheaper upgrade version. You'll find two discs in the box; 32-bit and 64-bit on separate DVDs. Check your computer's specifications (see page 209) if you don't know whether your system is 32- or 64-bit

2 Insert the Windows 7 disc, ignore the install screen if it opens. Go to **Start** and click **My Computer.** Right click on your CD/DVD drive and select **Explore**. In the Explorer window that opens, go to **support** and then **migwiz**. Double click on **migsetup.exe** to launch Windows Easy Transfer

3 Follow the wizard to back up all the personal files and settings, inserting an external USB memory stick where necessary (see page 184 for more on this)

4 You don't need to remove or uninstall your existing version of Windows first. With Windows Vista running, simply insert the correct 32-bit or 64-bit Windows 7 DVD into your computer's disc drive

5 An Autorun or Install Windows box should appear. Click on **Install Now** and then click on **Go online to get the latest updates**. Accept the licence terms and then click **Next**

6 When prompted to choose which type of installation you'd like to perform, select the **Custom (advanced)** option. You'll see a list of drives or partitions (the sections of your hard drive) on your PC – click to highlight the one with your existing Windows installation on it (this is usually the C: drive) and then click **Next**

7 The next few stages are automatic and may take anything from a few minutes to over an hour depending on your setup. Your PC will restart once or twice during this process; this is normal

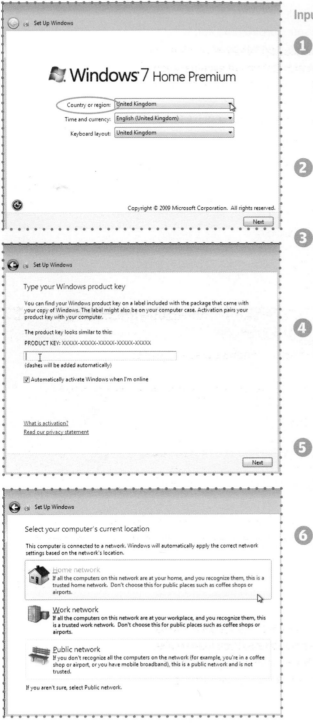

Inputting information

1 Eventually you'll be presented with a screen that allows you to select your region. Choose **United Kingdom** from the top drop-down menu and the time and currency and keyboard layout settings should change too. Click **Next**

2 In the next window, type a user name, change the suggested name for your PC as required and then click **Next**

3 Choose a password (we recommend a mixture of letters, numbers and a mixture of upper and lower case) and enter a hint in case you forget it, then click **Next**

4 In the following screen, enter the Windows 7 product key that came with your software (you'll find this printed on a sticker or a card inside the box – it's called the Product Key) and then click **Next**

5 Click **Use recommended settings** on the next screen and select your time zone from the drop-down menu on the following screen and then click **Next**

6 If you have a wireless network, you can click on your network, enter your security key and click **Next**. Both wired and wireless users will see a screen with three location options: Home, Work or Public

Finishing the installation

1 Windows will restart your computer and load up Windows 7 for the first time. This may take longer than a standard start-up but eventually you will see the Welcome screen followed by the Windows 7 desktop itself

2 To ensure your computer is properly protected, you must check for the latest updates from Microsoft (see page 198)

3 Finally, you need to put back all your old files and settings. You'll find a folder called 'Windows. old' on your C: drive. This usually contains user and program files from your previous Windows installation but the best way to put your files and settings back is to use the Windows Easy Transfer backup file we suggested you make earlier (see page 17). Simply insert the USB drive with the backup on it, double click the backup file you created earlier and follow the instructions

OPEN A PROGRAM

Once you've turned on your computer, the next step is to open a program. For example, you might want to open Microsoft Word to write a letter, or Internet Explorer to surf the internet.

There are two ways to do this. You can:

1 Double click on an icon on the desktop

2 The program will open in a new window

or:

1 Click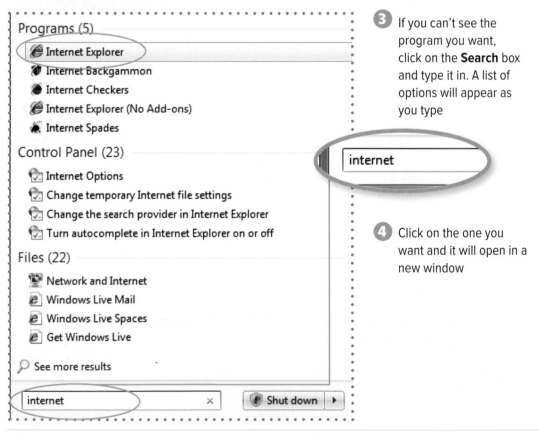

2 Select what you want to open from the list. For example, Email, Internet Explorer, Windows Media Player

TRY THIS

You can rearrange the icons on your desktop by right-clicking on a blank area, then clicking **Sort by**. You can choose to arrange them by name, size, type or date modified.

3 If you can't see the program you want, click on the **Search** box and type it in. A list of options will appear as you type

4 Click on the one you want and it will open in a new window

Programs (5)
- Internet Explorer
- Internet Backgammon
- Internet Checkers
- Internet Explorer (No Add-ons)
- Internet Spades

Control Panel (23)
- Internet Options
- Change temporary Internet file settings
- Change the search provider in Internet Explorer
- Turn autocomplete in Internet Explorer on or off

Files (22)
- Network and Internet
- Windows Live Mail
- Windows Live Spaces
- Get Windows Live

🔍 See more results

internet   ×   Shut down ▶

internet

CREATE A SHORTCUT

When you use Windows 7 for the first time, you will already have icons on the desktop for common programs. To add a desktop shortcut for another program:

1 Right click on a blank part of the desktop

2 In the menu that appears, hover your cursor over **New** (or click). A second menu will appear

3 Click **Shortcut**

4 Click **Browse** and select the program you want to create a shortcut for

---

◉ 🔲 Create Shortcut   **Browse...**

What item would you like to create a shortcut for?

This wizard helps you to create shortcuts to local or network programs, files, folders, computers, or Internet addresses.

Type the location of the item:

[   ] Browse...

Click Next to continue.

Next   Cancel

Jargon buster ▶

Icon
A small picture that represents an object or program.

5 Click **OK**

6 Click **Next**

7 Type a name for your shortcut – this can be the name of the program or your own made-up name

8 Click **Finish**

TIP
If you delete a shortcut, you're not deleting the actual program/folder, just the shortcut.

HANDLING WINDOWS

When you open a program or a web page, it will open as a window on your desktop. You can adapt these windows to the size you want and have more than one available to you at the same time.

CROSS ICON
This will close the window and you'll have to open the program afresh if you want to use it again. Depending on which program you're using, you may see two crosses – one for the file you're working on and one for the program as a whole. For example, in Microsoft Word, you will have the option to close either the document or Word completely.

MINIMISE ICON
Click and the window will disappear from the desktop, and is now accessible from the relevant icon in the taskbar.

MAXIMISE ICON
Click and the window will occupy the whole of the screen. Click again and your window will return to its original size.

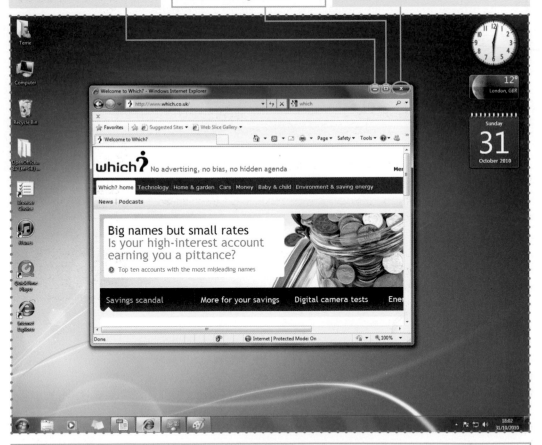

To alter the size of a window, hover near one side or the corner of the window until the pointer changes into a double-headed arrow, ◀▶ , click and drag the border up or down, or diagonally, to the size you want.

Snap You can view two windows side by side by dragging one off screen to the left, and the other to the right. Each window will instantly expand to take up half the screen.

TRY THIS

Programs that you have open will appear in the taskbar at the bottom of your screen. Hover your mouse cursor over one of the icons and you'll see a small preview of that window (you may see a number of previews if that program has more than one window or tab open).

Shake If you have a lot of windows on screen, shake the one you want to focus on (click on it and move the mouse cursor like you're shaking the window), and all of the other windows will be minimised. Shake the window again and the other windows will return.

NEXT STEP ▶

To learn more about the taskbar at the bottom of the screen, see page 24.

Peek To quickly look at your desktop, move your mouse over the transparent rectangle in the bottom right corner of your screen. This will make all of the windows on your screen turn transparent, so you can easily see gadgets and icons on your desktop. Click on the rectangle if you want to switch to the desktop view.

Main menus The Main Menu is generally the toolbar at the top of the program screen. A toolbar is a row, column, or block of buttons or icons representing tasks you can do within a program.

When you click on the words or tabs at the top of the screen they will open to reveal further options. Click on **Page Layout** in Microsoft Word, for instance, and you'll see options such as adding columns or altering the size of margins.

Page Layout

finding you way around

23

THE TASKBAR

The taskbar sits at the bottom of your desktop. You can open a number of programs at any one time and switch between them by clicking on the taskbar. When you minimise a window, it can also be reinstated at any time by clicking on it in the taskbar.

THE WINDOWS 7 START BUTTON
Click to open the main Windows menu (see page 7).

TASKBAR SHORTCUTS
These icons will always appear on your taskbar and allow you to easily access programs that you use often.

TASK BUTTONS
These are the programs that you have open. Hover over a button to get a preview of the windows that are open in that program.

NOTIFICATION AREA
Time, speaker volume, and icons that show status information, including the status of your internet connection. For example when you're printing, an icon will appear to show the status of the print job.

TIP
You can close a program by right-clicking on it in the taskbar and clicking **Close window**.

Resize the taskbar

You can resize the taskbar by following these instructions:

1 Right click on an empty space on the taskbar

2 A small window will appear. If **Lock the Taskbar** has a tick mark next to it, the taskbar is locked

3 Unlock it by clicking **Lock the Taskbar**. This will remove the tick

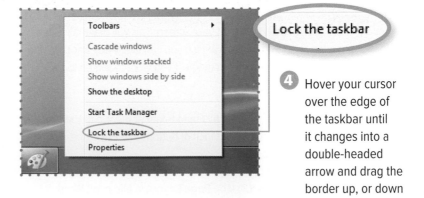

4 Hover your cursor over the edge of the taskbar until it changes into a double-headed arrow and drag the border up, or down

5 Drag the taskbar to the top or side of the screen to change its location

PINNING ITEMS TO THE TASKBAR

You can also choose what you have on your taskbar in the Taskbar Shortcuts section next to the Start button.

1 Click

2 Right click on any program

3 Click **Pin to Taskbar**

Pin to Taskbar

finding you way around

Jargon buster

Toolbar
A vertical or horizontal onscreen bar that's made up of small images; click these to perform commands.

Jargon buster

Taskbar
The bar running across the bottom of your screen from where you can open programs and access the main Windows functions.

TIP
Right click on a program icon in the taskbar to see a quick list of actions called a Jump list.

UNDERSTANDING THE CONTROL PANEL

From the Control Panel you can make changes to your computer, including the appearance of your desktop, your security settings and the programs that are on your computer.

To access the Control Panel:

1 Click

2 Click **Control Panel** in the right-hand column

SYSTEM AND SECURITY
View your computer's details and carry out tasks such as transferring or backing up your files. Also, from here you can check your computer's security status and see if any security updates are available (see page 201).

USER ACCOUNTS AND FAMILY SAFETY
Manage user accounts and set up parental controls (see page 33).

APPEARANCE AND PERSONALIZATION
Customise the appearance of your desktop and windows.

NETWORK AND INTERNET
Set up an internet connection, connect to a network and repair problems with your existing connection (see page 73).

HARDWARE AND SOUND
View information and make changes to devices, such as printers or speakers.

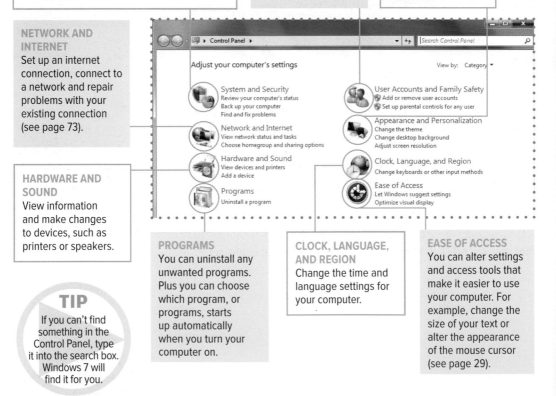

PROGRAMS
You can uninstall any unwanted programs. Plus you can choose which program, or programs, starts up automatically when you turn your computer on.

CLOCK, LANGUAGE, AND REGION
Change the time and language settings for your computer.

EASE OF ACCESS
You can alter settings and access tools that make it easier to use your computer. For example, change the size of your text or alter the appearance of the mouse cursor (see page 29).

TIP
If you can't find something in the Control Panel, type it into the search box. Windows 7 will find it for you.

TURNING YOUR COMPUTER OFF

When you've finished using your computer, there are a number of options for switching it off. Click on the arrow next to **Shut down** to reveal all of the options.

Shut down Your computer will switch off fully.

Switch user If somebody else wants to use the computer and has a user account, this will close your account and allow them to log on. You can then switch back if necessary.

Log off This will close your session and take you back to the log-in screen.

Lock This will close your session and take you back to the log-in screen. When you want to return to your session, you'll need to put in your password to resume (if you haven't set up a password, see page 204).

Restart Your computer will switch off and immediately start up again. You may have to do this after installing software.

Sleep Puts your computer into 'sleep mode'. This saves your session and puts your computer into a low power state. When you want to resume your session, press the **On** button on the front of your computer.

TIP
After programs/ updates have been installed, you'll often be prompted to restart your computer.

BE CAREFUL
Always shut down properly, as described above. Turning off your computer using the On/ Off button can cause problems the next time you start up.

NEXT STEP
For advice on PC security see page 198.

finding you way around

⏵ Customising your PC

PERSONALISE YOUR DESKTOP

To change the appearance of your desktop:

1 Right click anywhere on the desktop

2 Click **Personalize**

3 From this menu you can change how your screen looks

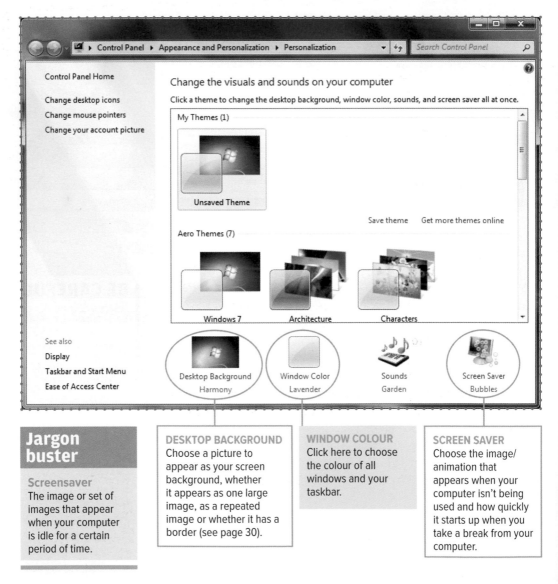

DESKTOP BACKGROUND Choose a picture to appear as your screen background, whether it appears as one large image, as a repeated image or whether it has a border (see page 30).	**WINDOW COLOUR** Click here to choose the colour of all windows and your taskbar.

SCREEN SAVER
Choose the image/ animation that appears when your computer isn't being used and how quickly it starts up when you take a break from your computer.

Jargon buster

Screensaver
The image or set of images that appear when your computer is idle for a certain period of time.

Ease of Access Center

Windows 7 has an Ease of Access Center, from where you can tweak or customise your settings. To launch this, click **Control Panel**, select **Ease of Access**, then **Ease of Access Center**.

Here are some tips on making your PC easier to use.

TRY THIS

If your desktop icons are disorganised, right click on the blank area of the desktop and click **Sort by**. You'll see various options for ordering your icons.

▶ Start Magnifier. This is a virtual magnifying glass and is helpful for tasks including typing documents or reading a news story online. Click **Start Magnifier** to zoom in on the screen. Move your mouse cursor to the edges of the screen to navigate around the page

▶ Make the computer easier to see. There are a number of options here that will make it easier to see things on screens. For example, you can make all the items on the screen larger by adjusting the colour and transparency of windows borders

▶ Make the mouse easier to use. Under the heading **Mouse pointers**, you can increase the size of the mouse cursor/pointer

NEXT STEP

You can create a screensaver with your own photos (see page 30).

customising your PC

▶ Customising your PC

CREATE YOUR OWN SCREENSAVER

BE CAREFUL

You can download screensavers from the internet, but watch out. Some may contain viruses or seriously slow down your computer. Only download from reputable sources – for example, sites that you're familiar with and know you can trust.

A screensaver appears when your computer is left idle for a certain period of time. You can select one of the generic screensavers or choose to use your own photos.

1 Right click anywhere on the desktop

2 Click **Personalize**

3 Click **Screensaver** and the screensaver window will appear

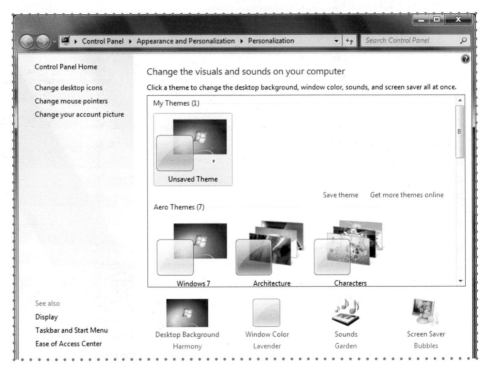

4 You can either choose a screensaver from the drop-down menu or create one from your own photos

5 To use your own photos, select **Photos** from the drop-down menu

NEXT STEP ▶

Find out how to organise your photos on page 156.

6 Click **Preview** to see what your new screensaver will look like – all your images will be displayed in sequence

ADJUST THE SETTINGS

1 You can adjust the length of time your computer will be inactive before your screensaver activates by selecting a time in the **Wait** box

2 A screensaver can be deactivated by using the keyboard or mouse. Tick the **On Resume** box next to the Wait box if you want to make sure that your password must be entered to access the computer at that point

3 To customise your screensaver further, click on **Settings**. When you're happy with your choices, click **OK**

ADD A SIDEBAR AND GADGETS

The sidebar is an area of the desktop that runs (by default) along the right-hand edge of the screen and plays host to your Gadgets – mini applications that run on your desktop at all times. These gadgets provide instant access to useful things like a clock or calculator as well as fun things like a mini-slideshow of your photos.

1 To add a gadget, right click on the desktop

2 Click **Gadgets.** You'll see a selection of gadgets you can choose from. Double click on a gadget to add it

3 To remove a gadget, click on the gadget you want to remove. Click on the cross icon to remove it

4 To move a gadget, click on the gadget you want to move. Click on the dotted icon

5 Drag and drop the gadget to the desired position

▶ Customising your PC

CREATE DIFFERENT USER ACCOUNTS

When you first set up your computer, Windows creates an Administrator account. This is an access-all-areas pass to your computer. Someone logged in on this account can install programs and make changes to the computer. If everyone that uses your computer has this level of access, it can cause problems. Plus, if you use this account as standard, it leaves you more open to security breaches.

Restricted user accounts – which was known as Standard accounts in Windows Vista – grant limited access to the computer. When you log into your user account, Windows knows which folders or files you may open, how you like your screen to look and what changes you're permitted to make to the computer. If you try to make a change you're not permitted to make, you'll be asked for the Administrator password.

TIP

To make changes to your user account at any time, click **Control Panel**, then **User Accounts** and select your account.

To create separate user accounts on your PC:

1 Click

2 Click on **Control Panel**, select **User Accounts and Family Safety**, then **Add or remove user accounts**

3 Click on **Create a new account**. Type in the user's name and select **Standard User**

4 Click **Create Account**

5 You can create a password by clicking on your new account and clicking **Create a password**

6 You can change the picture icon that's allocated to each user account by selecting an account and then clicking **Change the picture**

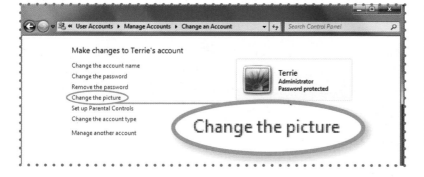

PARENTAL CONTOLS

1 If you want to limit how someone uses your computer, click **Set up Parental Controls** on the 'Manage account' page and select the account you want to restrict. Under **Windows Settings**, select what you'd like to control – for example, you can block websites or limit the time your child spends on the computer

2 When you've made your choices, select **On, enforce current settings**. Click **OK**

SWITCH BETWEEN USERS

To switch to a different user while you're using your computer:

1 Click

2 Click on the arrow icon next to 'Shut down'

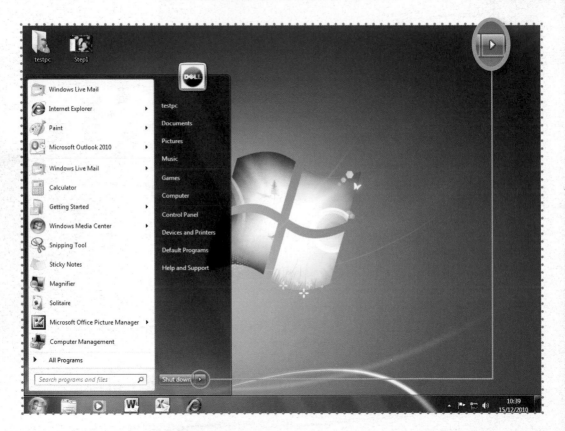

TRY THIS

You can also switch users by pressing **Ctrl, Alt** and **Delete** simultaneously, and then selecting from the drop-down menu as above.

3 From the drop-down list, click **Switch user**. Your programs won't be closed down; when you switch back to your user account, everything will be as you left it

4 Select the user account that you want to switch to

CREATING DOCUMENTS

By reading this chapter you will get to grips with:

 Using word processing software

Formatting documents

Creating a basic spreadsheet

OFFICE SUITES

An office suite is a package of programs that enables you to create, edit, read and manage a series of different documents. Generally, suites include a word processing and a spreadsheet program. They may also include a database program, presentation application, and a communication and personal organiser (email, calendar and contacts).

The software that came with your computer may contain a very basic word processor, such as Wordpad (that comes built into Windows), but investing in a proper office suite is something that almost every computer user should consider if they're going to make the most of their computer. Microsoft Office is one of several office suites available, and includes Microsoft Word and Microsoft Excel. Some other suites can even be downloaded for free, for example, OpenOffice at www.openoffice.org.

Microsoft Office is one of the most popular office suites, and for this reason, we've focused on Microsoft Word and Excel for this chapter.

CREATE A DOCUMENT

To open a new document in Word:

TIP
Files will usually be saved to your hard drive by default – this will show up as your C: drive.

1 Open Microsoft Word – there may be an icon on the desktop or taskbar. If not, search for it by clicking on the

2 A new blank document will open automatically. If you already have a document open, and want to start a new one, click **File**

3 Click **New**. In the list that appears, Blank document will automatically be highlighted

4 Click on the **Create** button. A new blank document will appear and you can begin typing

SAVE A DOCUMENT

 Click **File**, then click **Save**. If this is the first time you have saved your document, the **Save As** dialogue box will open

 The default location for saving files is the **Documents** folder. Word will also have given your document a file name based on the first few words in your document

 Click **Save** if you're happy with these defaults

Alternatively:

 If, as is more likely, you want to save your document somewhere different, you can browse to a different location by using the shortcuts on the left-hand side of the **Save As** dialogue box

 If you want to name your document yourself click in the **File name** box to highlight the name and type the name of your choice over the top of the default name

 Click **Save**. If you have saved your document previously but want to give it a new name, select **Save As** from the drop-down list

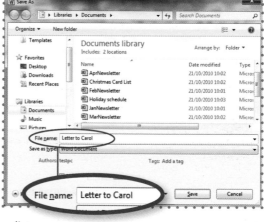

Save as an older format
If someone you've sent a file to can't open it, it may be because they have an older version of Word (Word 2007 and 2010 use the .docx file format and this isn't always compatible with earlier versions). To ensure your documents can be opened and read using previous versions of Microsoft Word:

 Follow points 1 and 2 above

 Click the down arrow on the right of where it says **Save as type**

 Select **Word 97 – 2003 Document** from the drop-down list. Click **Save**

> **TRY THIS**
> You can also save your work by clicking the small floppy disc icon in the top left of your screen – or by pressing the **Ctrl** and then **S** keys on your keyboard.

> **TRY THIS**
> If you try to close a document without saving, don't worry – a dialogue box will prompt you to save it. Click **Save** to save your document, **Don't Save** to lose any changes or **Cancel** to continue working on the document.

▶ Word

THE WORD RIBBON

The Ribbon acts as the main toolbar in Word and key functions are organised under tabs.

The Home tab

The basic formatting tools. From here, you can change the style, size and colour of your text, create bulleted and numbered lists and more. Find out how to use these on page 45.

The Insert tab

Insert other elements into your document such as charts, shapes and pictures (see page 50). You can also add headers and footers or the date and time.

The Page Layout tab

Change the orientation of your page from vertical (portrait – usually the default setting) to horizontal (landscape), create multiple columns of text or add borders to your page.

The References tab

A great tool for anyone writing long research documents or papers. Insert endnotes and footnotes into long documents or create a table of contents, and more.

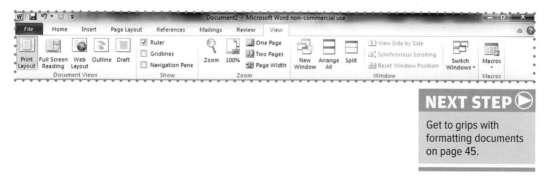

The Mailings tab

Create labels and envelopes, or do a mail merge.

Review

Check the contents of your document using the spellchecker (see page 51) or access the thesaurus. You can also Track Changes, which allows you to see the changes that you or others have made to a single document.

View

Zoom in or out on documents to make them easier to view. You can also see how your document will look printed out, published online or in other formats.

NEXT STEP ⊛

Get to grips with formatting documents on page 45.

PRINT A DOCUMENT

Open your document (see page 36), then follow these steps to print out your work with the default settings:

1 Click **File** in the toolbar

2 Click **Print**

3 You'll see a preview of what you are about to print on the right-hand side

4 Click the **Print** button

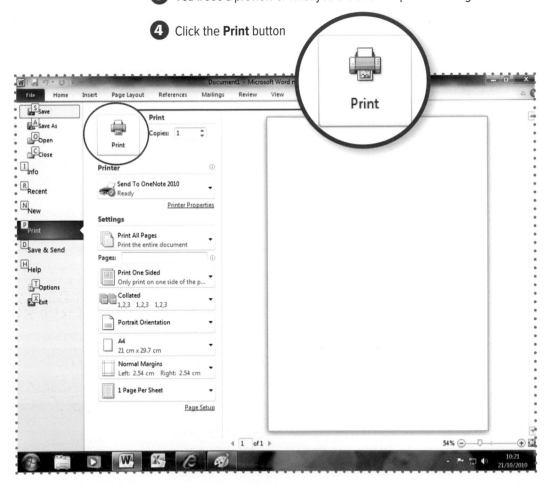

To pick a different printer or print style

1 To select a different printer, click the down arrow next to the current printer, and click instead on the one you want to use

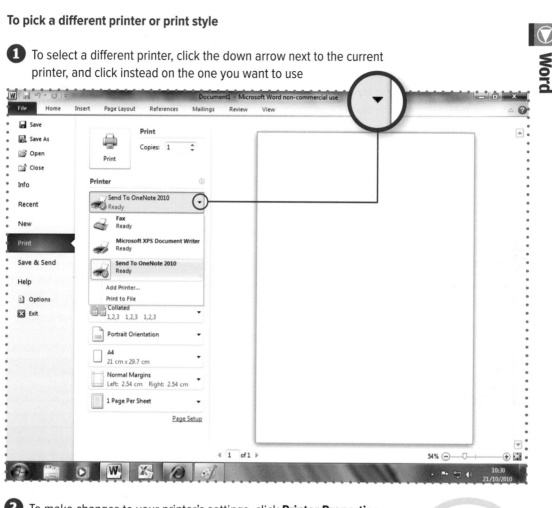

2 To make changes to your printer's settings, click **Printer Properties**, which is behind the drop down menu shown on the illustration above

3 Click **Advanced** for more options

4 Depending on your printer model, you may be able to select which tray of the printer the paper should come from, change the size of paper you print on, or opt for double-sided printing

5 Click **OK** when you're happy with the changes you've made

TIP

To go straight to the print menu, press **Ctrl + P**.

PRINT ERRORS EXPLAINED

Sometimes your document just doesn't print out as you want it to. Here are some of the more common printer errors.

I'm trying to print on both sides of the page to save on paper costs but the text is appearing upside down on the reverse of the paper.
How your printer handles double-sided printing will vary, and if it doesn't automate it in the printer (most don't), it's vital that you follow any onscreen instructions. Many printers have a helpful guide symbol inscribed on the paper tray, and you can use this to work out which way you need to insert the paper.

TIP
Some printers give you the option to print double-sided. This is sometimes referred to as duplex printing.

When I print a document, some of my text or images end up off the side of the page.
Start by checking the paper size option you're using. If you're using A4, click on **Properties** or **Printer Properties** when you try to print. Make sure it's set to A4 and not US Letter. In the Properties window you may also see options for Borderless Printing or Borderless Auto Fit. Selecting one of these should ensure that nothing is cropped off by the margins.

I want to print labels, but they keep coming out wrong. Can you help?
Ensure you're using the right template. Avery makes industry standard labels that are supported by the templates in Microsoft Word and Outlook – you can download the templates from Office Online when you create a new document. Most Avery alternatives list the Avery number they correspond to. Pick a template that lists the Avery label (or equivalent) that you're using in your printer.

The printer is printing gibberish and spitting out paper. What's going wrong?
If this happens with a single document, it probably isn't a problem with the printer. If it happens with all documents that you try to print, you may need to reload or update the software that runs your printer. Follow these instructions:

1 Disconnect your printer from the computer

2 On the computer, click

3 Click **Devices and Printers**

4 Right click on your printer

5 Select **Remove device**

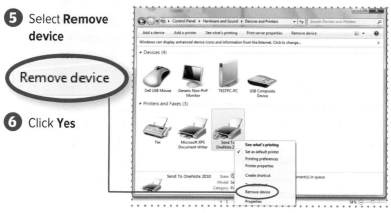

6 Click **Yes**

Then visit your printer manufacturer's website and download the latest available driver for your printer, making sure you choose the version appropriate to your version of Windows. Finally, follow the instructions to install and set up the software.

Jargon buster

Driver
Software that allows your computer to communicate with devices, such as a printer.

When I print a photo, the colours seem wrong or faded.

It's likely that your cartridges are running low or the ink nozzles are clogged. You'll need to print a test page:

1 Click

2 Click **Devices and Printers**

3 Right click on the printer you're using

4 Select **Properties**

5 On the first tab, usually called **General**, click the **Print Test Page** button. Alternatively you may have an option to click **Troubleshoot**

The test page will show samples of black, cyan, magenta and yellow ink. If one of these is missing or faded, switch off and switch on the printer at the power source so that it resets and self-cleans. Repeat the test page. If you still have problems, you may need to replace your old printer cartridge.

My document won't print because another printing task (or job) is clogging up the print queue.

Your printer software organises jobs into a queue and, if one job fails, this can prevent any other work from being done. To see the print queue follow these steps:

1 Click

2 Click **Devices and Printers**

3 Double click on your printer

4 The **Status** column should tell you if a job has failed and why

5 To delete the job and get the queue moving again, click on the relevant document

6 Click **Cancel** from the top menu and restart your computer (see page 27)

I've replaced my ink cartridge and now my printer isn't working.

Check that you removed any protective tape or film from the ink cartridge when you put it in your printer. Often the ink nozzles will be protected by a strip of tape, but the cartridge won't work with this fitted.

Also try switching the printer on and off at the power source and disconnecting then reconnecting the USB lead that connects your computer and printer. Finally, see if there are any indicators flashing on your printer. You may need to press the one that's flashing to get the printer online and back in action.

FORMAT A DOCUMENT

You can use Word's formatting tools to customise everything from the font, colour and size of individual text to the border of an image or the entire layout of your page. You can even apply new styles to the whole document at a time and it's possible to preview what many of your changes will look like before you actually commit to them.

Many common formatting tasks can be carried out using the tools under the **Home tab** in the top toolbar. The Home tools are grouped under **Font**, **Paragraph**, **Styles** and **Editing**. In the Font segment of the toolbar, you'll find several options for changing the look, size and style of your text. In each case you'll need to highlight the text you want to change first by clicking next to it and dragging your mouse over it.

SIMPLE TEXT FORMATTING

1 Highlight the text you want to alter

2 Click the **down arrow** next to the name of the current font in the toolbar to see a list of available fonts

3 Scroll through the list and preview what the font will look like by hovering your mouse cursor over its name (without clicking). The highlighted text in your document will change to the font, but not permanently

4 To actually make the change, click on your chosen font's name in the list

5 Clicking the **B**, **I** or **U** buttons in the **Font** section of the toolbar will change the text you have highlighted to bold, italic or underlined respectively

6 You can increase the font size (and preview your changes) by clicking the down arrow next to the current font size (the default font size is 12)

7 To change the colour of highlighted text, click the down arrow next to the **Font Colour** button (the one that features the letter 'A' underlined in red)

8 Hovering the mouse over a colour in the palette that appears will preview what your highlighted text will look like with that colour applied. Clicking on the colour will actually make the change

TIP
For more on highlighting text, see page 12.

FORMAT PARAGRAPHS

With the Paragraph section of the Home tab, you can customise the layout of your page.

Change alignment

1 By default, Word aligns text to the left-hand side of the page. You can change this to align to the left margin, centre your text, align to the right or, alternatively, justify your text in a block in the middle of your page

2 Select your text and click on one of the alternative alignment options in the Paragraph section of the **Home** toolbar

Make a bullet-pointed or numbered list

1 Type your list into the document, pressing **Enter** on your keyboard after each item so that they are all on a separate line

2 To add bullet points, highlight your list and click on the **down arrow** on the bullet point button

TRY THIS

To change spacing between your lines, highlight your paragraph, right click and select **Paragraph**. Click the drop-down menu below **Line Spacing** and select from the various options.

Jargon buster

Justified text
Justified text means that every line is spaced so that it's of equal length (flush with the right-hand margin as well as the left).

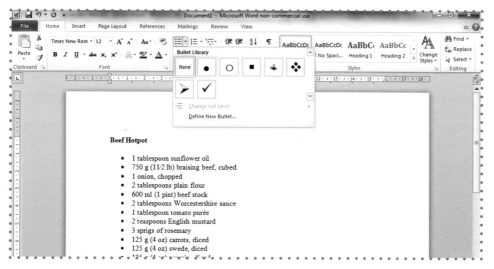

3 In the drop-down menu that appears, preview the different bullet styles by holding your mouse cursor over them

4 Click to select your choice. The same principle applies to numbering your list with the numbering icon

WORD TEMPLATES

Word comes with some useful templates and page layouts that you can use as the basis for a new document. To open a new document from one of Word's templates:

1 Click **File**

2 Click **New**

3 You will see a selection of available templates under the Home heading

4 Click on **Sample templates** to see a range of templates for letters, newsletters, CVs and more

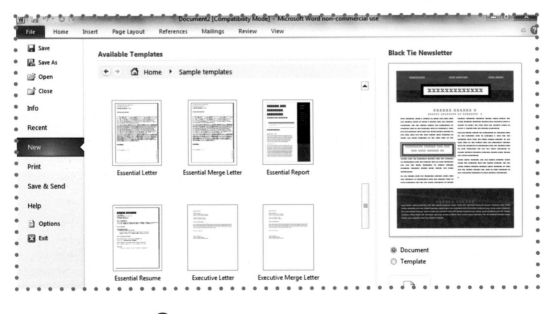

5 Once you've chosen your template, click on the **Create** button

ONLINE TEMPLATES

You can choose from a range of other templates from Microsoft Office Online (you will need to be connected to the web – see page 68). Simply follow these steps:

 Follow the instructions (opposite) to open a new Word template and, if you're connected to the internet, you'll see further templates under 'Office.com/templates' on the screen shown opposite

 Select one by clicking on it

3 Click **Download**

▶ Word

INSERT A PICTURE

1 Click once on the page at the point where you'd like the image to go

2 Click on the **Insert tab** on the top toolbar

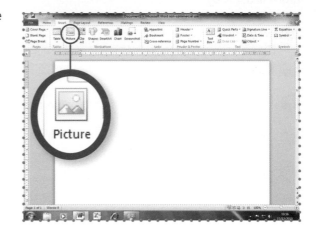

3 Click the **Picture** icon

4 Look for the image you want (see page 156) and double click on it to insert it

5 The Ribbon across the top will change, showing a number of borders that you can apply to your photograph. Click on a border if you want one

6 In the **Arrange** part of the Ribbon, you can change how the picture sits within the text, for example, in the centre. Highlight your image and click on the **Position** button. Hold your mouse over some of the options that appear to see where on your page your picture fits best. Click on the one you choose

Add a caption
You might want to add a caption to your picture:

1 Right click on the picture once it's in the document and select **Insert Caption**

2 A dialogue box will appear. Enter your caption in the box marked **Caption**

NEXT STEP ▶

To find out more about editing your pictures, see page 158.

3 Choose whether you want this to appear above or below your picture

4 Click **OK**

SPELLCHECK A DOCUMENT

If there's a spelling error in your document, a wavy red underlining will appear under it (grammatical errors are underlined with wavy green underlining).

To correct an individual spelling error:

1 Right click on the word

2 Select the correctly spelled version from the suggestions

To spellcheck a whole document:

1 Click the **Review** tab in the main toolbar

2 Click the **Spelling and Grammar** icon

TRY THIS

To change the default language that the spell check uses, click on the **Review** tab, click **Spelling & Grammar**, and then **Options**. Click on **Language** and choose the language you require. Click **OK**.

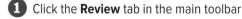

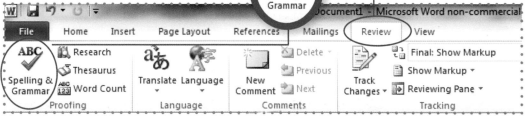

3 In the **Spelling and Grammar** dialogue box, Word will suggest possible corrections for each of the errors. You can accept Word's suggested correction by highlighting the one you want and clicking on the **Change** button

4 Alternatively, type your own correction over the incorrect text and click **Change**

5 You can reject Word's corrections – this is useful, for example, when Word doesn't recognise the spelling of a person's name, or a slang word you've used. Either click **Ignore Once** or **Ignore All** if you don't want the spellchecker to flag up recurring examples of the same word

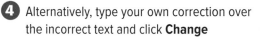

ORGANISE YOUR DOCUMENTS

Saving all of your documents loose in the Documents folder (see page 37) without an ordering system can make finding specific files a little unwieldy. It is worth organising them.

Create sub-folders

1 Click , then **Computer**

2 Click **Documents**

3 Right click and hover your mouse over **New**

4 Click **Folder** and give your new folder a name, for example 'Personal'

5 Press **Enter**

When you want to save a document here:

1 Click **File** and **Save As**

2 Click **Documents**

3 Click on the **Personal** folder icon and click **Save**

RENAME A FILE

1 Right click on the file you want to rename (you don't need to open it)

2 Click **Rename**

3 Type your new name

4 Press **Enter**

SELECT MULTIPLE FILES OR FOLDERS

You might want to select a number of files at the same time, for example, to delete, copy or print them all.

1 Open the folder that contains the files or folders you want to select

2 Hold down **Ctrl**

3 Click all the items you want to include

4 To change your selection at any point, just click a blank area of the folder window and start again

SEARCH FOR A LOST FILE

Windows has several default folders for storing files including Documents, Pictures and Music. Files are stored depending on the file type – for example, a .doc file will be stored in Documents, and a .jpeg file will be stored in Pictures. If you can't find a file, these folders are a good place to start your search. There are a few ways you can search for a missing document.

1 Click and enter text in the **Instant Search** box. As you type, files and applications that match what you're typing will appear automatically

2 Alternatively, click on **Pictures**, **Documents** or **Music** and a window will open where you can search for that particular file type

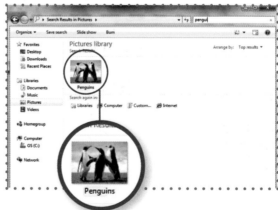

3 As you type, you will get the option to filter your search. With pictures for example, you can click on **Date taken** if you want to see files from a certain period

4 Or click **Tags** to locate pictures with a specific tag

 **Word**

WORD TIPS

Keyboard shortcuts

There are shortcuts for carrying out common tasks in Word so that you don't have to use your mouse and click on a number of buttons. The following two-key combinations might come in handy.

Ctrl + S to save a document
Ctrl + P to print a document
Ctrl + A to highlight the whole of your document

Or, highlight a specific word/words, then use:
Ctrl + I to italicise text
Ctrl + B to make text bold
Ctrl + U to underline text

Using the format painter

If you've already formatted text and want to apply those same effects to another paragraph:

1 Highlight the text you've already formatted

2 Select the **Home** tab on the **Office** Ribbon

3 Click on the **Format Painter** icon

4 Select the text you want to apply the formatting to by highlighting it, and it will automatically match the appearance of the text you originally highlighted

Use the highlighter pen

Word 2007 contains a high-tech version of a highlighter pen with which you can draw attention to key areas of text. To highlight a paragraph:

1 Select your text and select the underlined **abc** icon (on the **Home** tab)

2 Click the **down arrow** to choose the highlighter colour

Undo a mistake

It's easy to get carried away with the special effects. But don't panic if you've overdone it. Simply highlight the text in the normal way and click on the **clear formatting** icon (it resembles an eraser).

Create wider margins

When you launch a new Microsoft Word document, the Normal template applies the margin widths automatically. However, you can change these if, for instance, you want wider margins.

1 Select the **Page Layout** tab

2 Click on the **Margins** button

3 Click **Wide** to add bigger margins

Adding columns

Adding columns to a Word document is especially useful if you write a newsletter and want to give your document a magazine feel. To change the number of columns in your document:

1 Click the **down arrow** beneath the **Columns** icon (within the **Page Layout** tab)

2 Select the number of columns you require from the list that appears

Add a border

Borders are a useful feature to add to a newsletter or party invite.

1 Select the **Page Layout** tab

2 Click on the **Page Borders** icon

3 On the **Page Border** tab, choose your preferred border style (**Box**, **Shadow**, **3D** or **Custom**). You will see a preview of what your choice will look like in the right-hand side of the window as you click on it

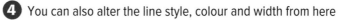

4 You can also alter the line style, colour and width from here

5 Click **OK** when you're happy with your choices

Using special effects
Add a touch of pizzazz to your document with some special effects:

1 Highlight your text

2 Click the arrow next to the **Special Effects** icon to get a drop-down menu

3 Click on a special effect to apply shadows or outlines to your text

4 You can also open the Effects menu by clicking on **Effects** in the main toolbar

Turn your page from portrait to landscape
It can be useful to flip your page on its side (from portrait to landscape) if you have a wide table to insert in your document. To do this:

1 Select the **Page Layout** tab on the **Word** Ribbon

2 Click the drop-down arrow underneath **Orientation**

3 Click the **Landscape** icon. You can change it back the same way

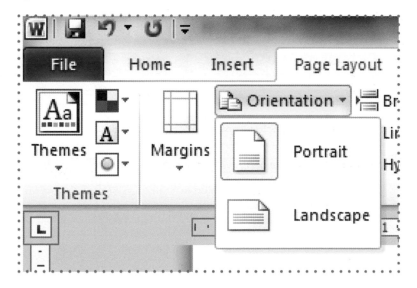

EXCEL EXPLAINED

A spreadsheet application such as Microsoft Excel lets you organise information into columns and rows. This is useful for bookkeeping and accounting, and for arranging complicated information into tables and grids.

The Ribbon (main toolbar) features the most common Excel functions split into groups such as Font (for basic text editing functions) and Alignment (for controlling text layout).

A cell address is identified by the letter of the column and the number of the row in which it sits. The highlighted cell in our example is B12, for example.

An Excel file is known as a workbook. It contains a number of spreadsheets (called worksheets). Each worksheet is full of rectangular boxes known as cells and each cell has its own reference or cell address.

Personal budget1 [Compatibility Mode]

File Home Insert Page Layout Formulas Data Review View

Tahoma 10 A A Custom

Paste B I U

Clipboard Font Alignment Num

B12 fx =SUM(B6:B11)

Personal budget

	A	B	C	D
1	**Personal budget**			
2				
3		Jan	Feb	March
4	**EXPENSES**			
5	**Daily living**			
6	Groceries	80.00	95.00	80.00
7	Child care	50.00	50.00	50.00
8	Dry cleaning	10.00	0.00	20.00
9	Dining out	55.00	0.00	60.00
10	Housecleaning service	25.00	25.00	25.00
11	Dog walker	5.00	5.00	5.00
12	**Daily living totals**	**225.00**	**175.00**	**240.00**
13				
14	**Transportation**			
15	Gas/fuel	20.00	30.00	30.00
16	Insurance	30.00	30.00	30.00
17	Repairs	0.00	20.00	0.00
18	Car wash/detailing services	0.00	0.00	0.00
19	Parking	20.00	25.00	20.00
20	Public transportation	10.00	10.00	10.00
21	**Transportation totals**	**80.00**	**115.00**	**90.00**
22				
23	**Entertainment**			
24	Cable TV	20.00	20.00	20.00
25	Video/DVD rentals	5.00	0.00	5.00
26	Movies/plays	10.00	0.00	10.00

Personal budget

Ready

Numerical formulae can also be applied in Excel to perform specific mathematical calculations. Excel can also quickly and easily convert information contained in a spreadsheet into a graph or chart.

Further Ribbon tabs – such as Insert, Page Layout, Formulas and Data – provide access to more advanced or specialised options.

You can sort data within a range of cells, in alphabetical or numerical (and ascending or descending) order.

The formula bar allows you to make mathematical calculations using the data you've entered in the cells of your spreadsheet (see page 66).

	May	June	July	Aug	Se
	80.00	80.00	75.00	60.00	
	50.00	50.00	50.00	50.00	
	20.00	50.00	0.00	0.00	
	40.00	30.00	50.00	50.00	
	25.00	25.00	0.00	0.00	
	5.00	5.00	5.00	5.00	
	220.00	**240.00**	**180.00**	**165.00**	
	20.00	20.00	20.00	20.00	
	30.00	30.00	30.00	30.00	
	100.00	0.00	120.00	0.00	
	0.00	0.00	0.00	0.00	
	20.00	20.00	20.00	30.00	
	10.00	10.00	10.00	10.00	
	180.00	**80.00**	**200.00**	**90.00**	
	20.00	20.00	20.00	20.00	
	5.00	0.00	10.00	5.00	
	0.00	20.00	10.00	0.00	

TRY THIS

Like Word, you can highlight elements of your document – a particular row or column, say – and then move your mouse over certain formatting options to get a preview of what they would look like (see page 46).

Excel

CREATE A BASIC SPREADSHEET

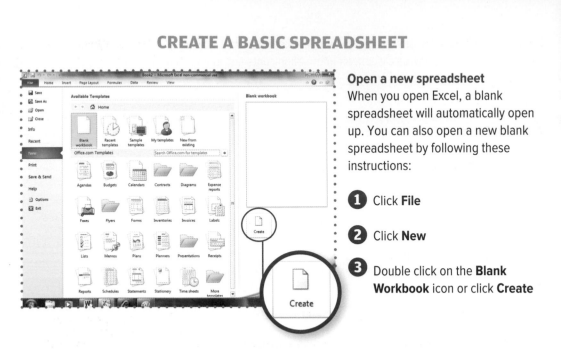

Open a new spreadsheet
When you open Excel, a blank spreadsheet will automatically open up. You can also open a new blank spreadsheet by following these instructions:

1 Click **File**

2 Click **New**

3 Double click on the **Blank Workbook** icon or click **Create**

Enter data into a spreadsheet
A spreadsheet is made up of individual blocks known as cells. To enter a piece of data (how much you spent on your mortgage, say) click on a cell and type in your data. Cells are identified by row numbers and column letters such as A1 or D14. You can also enter headings for your data in the same way – click on a cell and type in a title.

Adjust column width and row height
Your columns may not be wide enough to display all the text you have typed into them, so move your mouse to the top of the document so that it is pointing to the line between the A and B columns.

TRY THIS
You can sort data within a range of cells, in alphabetical or numerical (and ascending or descending) order. Click on **Sort & Filter** on the toolbar for more options.

Your cursor will change to a bold line with arrows pointing left and right. Click and drag the line to the width of the column you want on the left of the line. Then let go. You can also do the same for a single row – drag down to the depth you want in the row above.

You can also set values for the column width and row height for your whole spreadsheet at once:

1 Press **Ctrl** + **A** on your keyboard to select all of the spreadsheet

2 Select the **Home** tab

3 Click **Format** in the **Cells** section

 Format ▾

4 Select **Column Width** (or **Row Height**)

5 A small box will pop up displaying the current column width
(8.43 points by default; row height is 12.75 by default)

6 Enter the value that you require

7 Click **OK**

Add a £ sign

If you're using your spreadsheet to manage your household budget
or other expenses, you'll want to add £ signs to some of your figures.
Here's how:

1 Select the numbers the change should apply to, then click **Format** in
the **Cells** section

2 From the drop-down menu, click **Format Cells** at the bottom of
the list

3 Click **Currency** (in left-hand menu).
Use the up and down arrows to select
your preferred number of decimal
places in the small box on the right.
You can also change the currency
symbol, if necessary

4 Click **OK**

TRY THIS

The figures you enter
don't have to be
monetary amounts. You
can also enter figures for
years, hours, etc. Use the
same steps as adding
a £ sign, but click on a
different format.

CUSTOMISE YOUR SPREADSHEET

You can customise a document by adding borders, changing background and text colours and choosing new fonts.

Centre text

You may want to centre the text in some of your cells – for example, if they're column headings or titles.

1 Select the cells, columns or rows where you want the text to be centred

2 Right click anywhere in the selected area and select **Format cells**

3 Click the **Alignment tab**

4 Under **Text Alignment**, click the drop-down box under **Horizontal** and select **Center**. This will align the text in the first row to the centre of each cell of the spreadsheet

Center

Format Cells

| Number | Alignment | Font | Border | Fill | Protection |

Text alignment

Horizontal:

Center ▼ Indent: 0

Vertical:

Bottom ▼

☐ Justify distributed

Text control

☐ Wrap text
☐ Shrink to fit
☐ Merge cells

Right-to-left

Text direction:

Context ▼

Orientation

Text ——◆

0 ▼ Degrees

OK   Cancel

Change font, colour of text or background

① Follow points 1 and 2 opposite

② Click the **Font** tab and select the required font from the list. You can also customise the size, type and colour here

Format Cells

| Number | Alignment | Font | Border | Fill | Protection |

Font:
Calibri

Cambria (Headings)
Calibri (Body)
Agency FB
Aharoni
Algerian
Andalus

Font style:
Regular

Regular
Italic
Bold
Bold Italic

Size:
11

8
9
10
11
12
14

Underline:
None

Color:

☑ Normal font

Effects
☐ Strikethrough
☐ Superscript
☐ Subscript

Preview

AaBbCcYyZz

This is a TrueType font. The same font will be used on both your printer and your screen.

OK   Cancel

③ To change the cell background colour, ensure the cells you want to change are highlighted, click the **Fill** tab and select a colour of your choice from the palette below **Cell Shading**. Only the selected area will be shaded in the new colour

④ To change the colour for the rest of the cells (single cells, or whole columns/rows), select them separately and do the same

⑤ Click **OK** to see your changes

Add a border

 Follow points 1 and 2, opposite

 Click the **Border** tab

 Under Presets click the **Inside** option

 Click **OK**

Freeze Panes

When scrolling down a spreadsheet, you can lose sight of the headings at the top of the page, and it can be annoying to keep scrolling back up again to view them. To keep selected rows or columns in place while you scroll through the rest of the document:

1 Select the row below the one you'd like to freeze

2 Click **View**

3 Click **Freeze Panes** and then click **Freeze Top Row**

4 Next time you scroll down, the selected area will always appear at the top

5 To unfreeze, click **Unfreeze Panes**

Group data

Grouping data allows you to hide certain rows or columns of data (if you only want to see a summary of all the bills you pay, for example, rather than each individual one). To group data:

1 Select the row or column you want to hide

2 Select **Data** tab on the top toolbar

3 Click **Group**, then click **Group** again on the drop-down menu

4 Click the minus sign beneath the black outline bar to hide the data

5 Click on the plus sign when you want to show it again

NEXT STEP▶

Want your spreadsheet to do some calculations for you? Find out how to use formulae on page 66.

ADD UP A COLUMN OF FIGURES

You can use a formula to make calculations based on what you've entered into your spreadsheet. Here's how to add up a column or row of figures:

1 Highlight the row or column of figures you want to add up by clicking on the first one, holding down the mouse button and dragging it, letting go when you reach the last one, so that you've highlighted all the cells you want

2 Click on the **AutoSum** Σ button (under **Editing** in the **Home** tab toolbar)

3 The total sum of all the values in your selection will be displayed in the cell directly underneath the value for your final, highlighted cell, in this case January's living expenses (i.e. cell B12)

TRY THIS

If you select the blank cell under a list of numbers, then click **AutoSum**, Excel will highlight the numbers it thinks you want to add together. Click **AutoSum** again or press **Enter** to complete the calculation.

Excel

| B12 | fx =SUM(B6:B11) | | | | | | | |
A	B	C	D	E	F	G	H	I
Personal budget								
	Jan	Feb	March	April	May	June	July	Aug
EXPENSES								
Daily living								
Groceries	80.00	95.00	80.00	120.00	80.00	80.00	75.00	60.00
Child care	50.00	50.00	50.00	50.00	50.00	50.00	50.00	50.00
Dry cleaning	10.00	0.00	20.00	0.00	20.00	50.00	0.00	0.00
Dining out	55.00	0.00	60.00	65.00	40.00	30.00	50.00	50.00
Housecleaning service	25.00	25.00	25.00	25.00	25.00	25.00	0.00	0.00
Dog walker	5.00	5.00	5.00	5.00	5.00	5.00	5.00	5.00
Daily living totals	**225.00**	**175.00**	**240.00**	**265.00**	**220.00**	**240.00**	**180.00**	**165.00**
Transportation								
Gas/fuel	20.00	30.00	30.00	20.00	20.00	20.00	20.00	20.00
Insurance	30.00	30.00	30.00	30.00	30.00	30.00	30.00	30.00
Repairs	0.00	20.00	0.00	0.00	100.00	0.00	120.00	0.00
Car wash/detailing services	0.00	0.00	0.00	0.00	0.00	0.00	0.00	0.00
Parking	20.00	25.00	20.00	30.00	20.00	20.00	20.00	30.00
Public transportation	10.00	10.00	10.00	10.00	10.00	10.00	10.00	10.00
Transportation totals	**80.00**	**115.00**	**90.00**	**90.00**	**180.00**	**80.00**	**200.00**	**90.00**
Entertainment								
Cable TV	20.00	20.00	20.00	20.00	20.00	20.00	20.00	20.00
Video/DVD rentals	5.00	0.00	5.00	0.00	5.00	0.00	10.00	5.00
Movies/plays	10.00	0.00	10.00	0.00	0.00	20.00	10.00	0.00

WRITE A SIMPLE FORMULA

Excel's mathematical skills aren't confined to addition. So, if you want to find out how much money you've got left to spend after subtracting your outgoings from your income, for example, Excel can help.

The formula is an important part of the Excel spreadsheet. Formulae are mathematical operations used to perform a calculation. An Excel formula always starts with an = sign, and uses cell references to identify data to be included in the calculation. The most-used operations are:

- = minus
+ = plus
* = multiply
/ = divide
, = plus, but not consecutive

A typical formula might therefore be =(D6-F4)*G8 (the asterisk represents multiplication).

At first glance, these formulae can seem complicated, but stick with it. Excel formulae follow the standard order of mathematical operations we all learnt at school – hence the brackets to indicate the part of the calculation that needs to be performed first. The formula bar shows the address of the selected cell on the left-hand side.

To calculate something

TIP
You can add a row or column of figures by clicking on the autosum icon (see page 65).

1 Click on the cell where you want the answer to your calculation to appear

2 Enter your formula in the formula bar – for example, =C4-C34

3 Press **Enter**. The answer will appear in the cell you selected. When you make changes to the cells within the formula – in this instance, C4 and C34 – it will automatically recalculate the new figure

USING THE INTERNET

By reading this chapter you will get to grips with:

Setting up a broadband connection

Surfing the internet

Buying items online

YOUR INTERNET OPTIONS

To connect to the internet, you need a modem (and/or router), a phone line and an account with an internet service provider (ISP). A modem is a small, box-shaped device, which is connected at one end to your PC and the other to your phone line. Most new computers now come with a built-in modem. The modem connects via the phone line to another modem at the ISP. The modems talk to each other, sending information back and forth to your computer. This used to involve a dial-up connection on your phone line, but most people now connect to the internet using broadband. It provides a much faster service and you can use the phone and be online at the same time. There are three types of broadband.

Fixed ADSL broadband

Available to more than 99 per cent of UK households, ADSL (asymmetric digital subscriber line) broadband requires a fixed BT phone line. However, BT is not the only choice of broadband provider – ISPs such as TalkTalk use BT's network and offer their own broadband packages. ISPs also offer local loop unbundling (LLU). This is a type of ADSL broadband where ISPs install their own equipment in BT exchanges.

Advertised ADSL download speeds typically range from 0.5 to up to 20 megabits per second (Mbps). The speed you'll actually get, however, depends on a number of factors, including your distance from the phone exchange and the number of other people using your local BT exchange.

Pros
- ▶ Good choice of providers and packages
- ▶ Speeds are increasing and prices are dropping

Cons
- ▶ Some limitations on speed
- ▶ You have to pay a fixed-phone line rental

Who is it for?
Anyone with a fixed BT line who wants choice in providers and packages.

Cable broadband

Offered only by Virgin Media at the time of writing, cable broadband is an equivalent service to ADSL. It is available to around 50 per cent of UK homes, mostly in urban areas. You don't need a BT line, but may need to have a Virgin phone line installed.

Cable broadband has potentially faster download speeds than ADSL and can even get as high as 50Mbps. Your distance from the exchange won't affect the broadband speed you receive, but don't rely on getting advertised speeds as these are still affected by equipment or traffic at peak times. Virgin offers some cheap deals to cable customers taking two or more services (broadband, home phone, digital TV and mobile).

Pros
▶ Speed isn't affected by distance from exchanges
▶ Cable fibre quality means the potential speed is higher than ADSL
▶ Competitively priced packages

Cons
▶ Only available to half of UK households
▶ Only one choice of provider

Who is it for?
Price-conscious consumers in search of a cheap deal or those living a fair distance from a BT exchange but want to achieve fast broadband speeds.

Mobile broadband
Mobile broadband means the ability to connect to the internet wherever you're using your computer. By plugging a USB modem (dongle) into your computer's USB port, your computer can connect to the internet using a wireless data connection such as a 3G mobile signal.

Pros of mobile broadband
▶ You can surf the mobile internet wherever there's a 3G mobile signal
▶ You don't have to pay for fixed phone line rental
▶ Some companies offer pay-as-you-go (PAYG) mobile broadband so you don't have to tie yourself in to a lengthy contract

Cons of mobile broadband
▶ Maximum mobile broadband speeds aren't yet as fast as traditional fixed-line broadband
▶ The amount of data (such as music, text files, video and films) that you can download from the internet is capped at a fairly low level, and exceeding this can be very expensive
▶ Like for like, mobile internet access is more expensive than most fixed-line broadband contracts

NEXT STEP ⊚

If you are not happy with your existing broadband ISP, find out how easy it is to switch on page 82.

▶ Getting Connected

GET ADSL BROADBAND

If you're not already connected to the internet, follow these steps to get ADSL broadband:

 Find out if ADSL broadband is available in your area. Use a friend's internet connection to visit the website www.broadbandchecker. co.uk. Type in your postcode to see the options that are available in your area. Alternatively, phone a broadband provider and ask

 Phone your chosen broadband provider to discuss which package best suits your needs

 Ask them what speed you can expect to get and if there are any contract conditions – such as a cap on how much you can download. Also check their pricing structure. If your computer doesn't come with a built-in modem, ask whether they will provide a router or modem as part of the deal

 Once you've signed the contract, your line will be remotely activated so that it can carry ADSL broadband and voice calls at the same time. This may take about a week to be done

⑤ Once your line has been activated, you'll need to connect your router or modem and configure your computer following instructions on a CD sent to you by the ISP (see page 73)

Getting broadband if you already have dial-up internet

① Choose a broadband provider and find out from them how long it will take for broadband activation

② Cancel your dial-up internet subscription, timing it so you're not left without internet access for long

③ Ask your chosen broadband provider to activate your broadband, then install your modem and configure your computer as explained on page 73

CHOOSING A BROADBAND PROVIDER

With so many broadband providers out there, choosing which one is right for you can be a difficult decision. Consider the following:

Cost You don't pay for the time spent online. Broadband services start from £10 a month up to a maximum of around £35; prices vary according to the connection speed you opt for and how much data you download or upload.

Start-up costs You may need to pay up front for broadband line activation (around £25–£50), though some ISPs waive these fees in return for tying you to a 12-month contract. Some also throw in a free broadband modem or router in exchange for a 12- or 18-month contract, though you may have to return this if you switch provider within that time.

Speed Up to 8Mbps is the norm with most ISPs, though several are introducing speeds of up to 16 or 24Mbps in some areas. In practice, most people will find speeds of 1 or 2Mbps are adequate for surfing the internet and sending emails. But, if you want to download films, watch TV online or play games online, you'll see the benefits of a faster broadband speed.

Availability If you live in a rural area, you're more likely to run into difficulties getting a decent broadband service. Those living in urban or highly populated area have a better choice of providers and broadband packages.

Contracts Many broadband ISPs insist you sign up for 12 or even 18 months, so make sure you check this. Some do offer one-month contracts – but you'll usually have to pay for broadband equipment and connection up front. If you want to end a contract early, you normally have to pay a cancellation fee.

Usage limits Most ISPs put a limit on how much internet data you can download and upload – anything from 1 to 75 gigabytes (GB) a month. 1GB a month, for example, would let you surf the internet for two hours a day, send and receive 100 emails a week, and download 30 music tracks a week. But downloading or streaming TV or film can really bump up your broadband usage and many ISPs charge for exceeding the limit. Costs for this typically range from around £1 to £2 for each extra GB.

TRY THIS

Check your broadband speed at www.speedtest.net or www.thinkbroadband. com – though remember that your broadband speed results may vary by time of day, and accuracy will be affected by anything else you're doing on the computer.

BE CAREFUL

What you pay for isn't necessarily what you get. Many broadband customers find they get speeds well short of those advertised. Factors such as distance from the BT exchange, demand and traffic play a part in reducing broadband speeds.

⊳ Getting Connected

Fair usage policies If you opt for a home broadband service with no limits, check the ISP's 'fair usage policy'. If you abuse this, it may result in warning letters, restricted broadband speed or, at worst, a cancelled service. You'd have to try pretty hard to exceed most broadband fair usage limits, though. For example, AOL Broadband gives the following examples of excess downloading in a single month: more than 12,000 music tracks, more than 30,000 high-quality photos or around 60 movies.

Technical help Check how much it costs to call your ISP's technical helpline. Prices range from free to 10p a minute from a landline. If you run into difficulties, you'll be glad you have a free or low-cost technical helpline.

Go for a bundle Many ISPs offer big discounts on their broadband services if you take them as part of a bundle with other home phone, TV and mobile services. Some even offer 'free' home broadband if you sign up for other services at the same time. Check to see if there are hidden costs to this so-called 'free' broadband, such as broadband connection fees, download and upload usage restrictions and lengthy broadband contract.

TIP
Check what broadband speed your phone line can support before signing up. Go to www.dslchecker. bt.com/adsl.

GET SET UP

To connect to the internet, you need a modem and usually a router. A modem is a device that allows a computer to send information over a telephone line. It acts as a bridge between your computer and the modem at the ISP. A router is a device that splits that connection up so it can be used on more than one computer at home.

Set up your router

Once you've signed up with an ISP, most likely you will be sent a booklet/CD that helps you to set up your internet connection. For a router with an in-built modem, it's likely to include these steps:

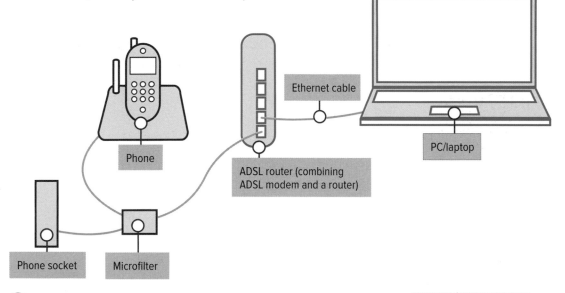

Phone

Ethernet cable

PC/laptop

ADSL router (combining ADSL modem and a router)

Phone socket

Microfilter

1 Attach a microfilter to the main phone socket (where the phone line enters the house)

2 All the cables you need should be included in the box with the router. Plug one end of the modem cable into the relevant microfilter socket. Plug the other end into the back of your router

3 Your telephone plugs into the microfilter too. This means that you can be on the phone while also having an active broadband connection

4 Connect your router's power supply and switch it on

Ethernet
A cable commonly used to connect a computer to a modem for internet access.

getting connected

⊳ Getting Connected

Connect your router to the computer

1 The easiest way to set up your router is to connect it to your PC or laptop via an ethernet cable (this will come in the router box)

2 Put one end of the ethernet cable into the socket on the PC and the other end into one of the four identical sockets on the router

Accessing your router's setup

1 Start up your computer and open your web browser to access your router settings

2 Enter the address of your router into the browser's address bar. This is a number listed in your manual. In the case of many routers, this number is 192.168.1.1 or 192.168.2.1

3 Press **Enter**

4 You will then be asked for login details. Your default username and password will be in your manual

Change your settings

 1 You'll see a page that looks like a web page – this is the router setup page. From here you can make changes to the router

Jargon buster

Microfilter
A device that attaches to your telephone socket and enables you to make voice calls and use broadband at the same time, via ADSL.

2 To change the default password, click the **Administration** tab, enter a password in the password window, confirm it and slick **save**

3 For the router to connect to the internet you need to configure the ADSL part of it with the right settings. Click on the **Setup** tab

4 The router will ask for your ISP user name and password. Enter these – again, they should have been provided by your ISP

5 You may be asked to enter details about 'encapsulation' or 'multiplexing'. You don't need to know what these mean. Simply ask your ISP about what you should see in these settings

6 Scroll down and save your changes

7 You should now be able to connect to the internet on the PC connected to the router. If you don't want to connect any PCs wirelessly, then you're done. If you do, continue to page 80

SET UP WIRELESS BROADBAND

Having set up your broadband connection with cables (see page 73), you can choose to go wireless if your router supports it. This means that your PC doesn't have to be physically connected in order to use broadband. Wireless networks use a type of radio wave to transmit data between machines, removing the need for cables.

Set up a wireless network

To set up a wireless (Wi-Fi) network, you'll need a central wireless router plus a wireless adaptor for each of the PCs or devices you want to connect. Many computers, particularly laptops, are already wireless enabled. If not, the easiest method is to plug in a USB adaptor. You can buy one of these small devices from a computer shop.

 In the router set-up page, click the **Wireless** tab

 In the **Network Name (SSID)** field change the name of your network to something memorable like 'Home wireless'

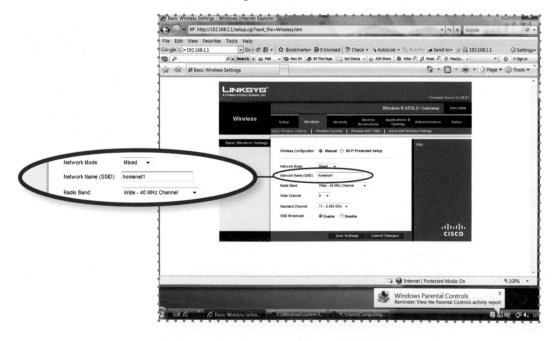

3 Choose the **Wireless Security** option. From here you can turn on security for your new wireless network

4 Select **WPA** from the drop-down menu and enter a pass phrase (this works the same as a password)

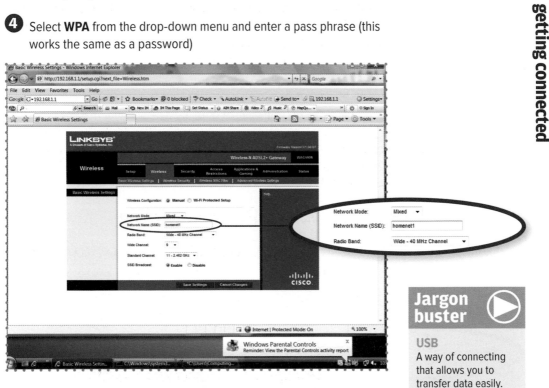

Jargon buster

USB
A way of connecting that allows you to transfer data easily. Many devices are connected to a computer via a USB cable.

5 Save your settings. For more on securing your wireless network, see page 78

6 Your computer should automatically detect any wireless network within its range. Click on the pop-up message and you will see a list of available wireless networks. On the list should be the network you named earlier, in this case 'Home wireless'

7 Select your wireless network from the list

8 You'll be prompted to enter your security pass phrase. Once you've done this, you'll be connected to your wireless network and can surf the internet

SECURE YOUR WIRELESS NETWORK

Wireless networks are far more convenient than traditional, wired ones, but they bring with them certain security risks. It's important that you take precautions to stop people connecting to your network, or even changing your network settings, without your knowledge.

▶ All wireless networks have a name (sometimes called the SSID) that you can change when you set up your router. Make it something that doesn't give any clues to your identity, or to the type of router that you're using

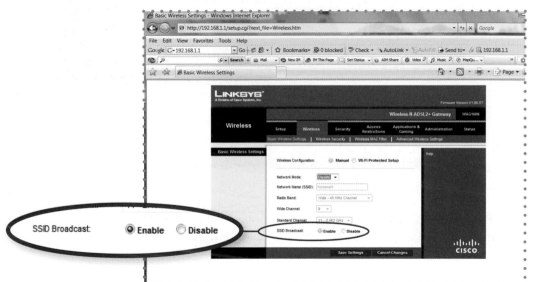

▶ If your router doesn't broadcast the network name (or SSID), it is more difficult for anyone looking for a network to connect to it. If you won't often be connecting new devices to your network, consider turning off the router's broadcast SSID option

▶ Many routers come with weak passwords like 'admin', which are easy for other people to guess. Change it to something more difficult

▶ Encrypt your network to make it more secure. Your router instruction manual should show you how

▶ If your computer is close to the router, then why not connect via cables? Turn off the wireless network from the router and nobody else will be able to connect wirelessly

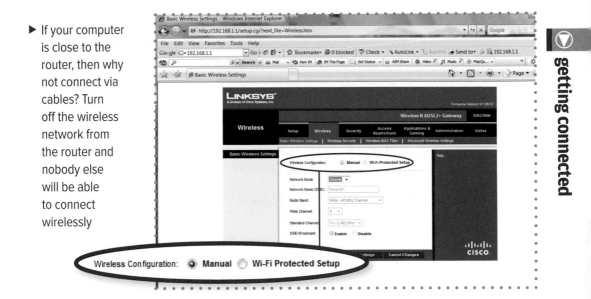

TIPS ON USING YOUR ROUTER

▶ Get the router working with a wired connection, using an ethernet cable before setting up wirelessly

▶ Remember that you can reset the router to its original settings if you make a mistake or forget the setup password. You can usually do this by holding down the reset button for a count of 10 seconds

▶ Connect the router to the phone socket that's nearest to where the line enters your house. Any additional distance can reduce signal quality and may affect your broadband connection

▶ Don't forget to install microfilters in your telephone sockets. Every device in your house that's connected to a phone socket (including phones and faxes) will need one

▶ Give your network a name that won't reveal your identity, location, or the make of your router

▶ Your router will be able to tell you all sorts of information about what it's doing. Clicking on the Status tab will let you see, for instance, whether your ADSL connection is active, and at what speed, or which computers are connected

CONNECT TO OTHER COMPUTERS

When multiple computers are connected, it's often referred to as a home network. You can share all kinds of data over a network – from documents and emails to music, photos and video. If you have a broadband internet connection, a network means that all the computers in your household can access the web at the same time.

Once you've set up your wireless broadband connection on one computer (see page 76), you're ready to connect other computers.

Install your wireless adaptors

 Each PC will need its own wireless adaptor and the setup procedure will differ depending on the make, model and type of adaptor

 During the setup procedure, follow onscreen instructions, making sure that you put a tick next to **Infrastructure Mode** and that you enter the name (SSID) of your wireless network

TIP
Many laptops will already be wirelessly enabled, so you won't need an adaptor to get online.

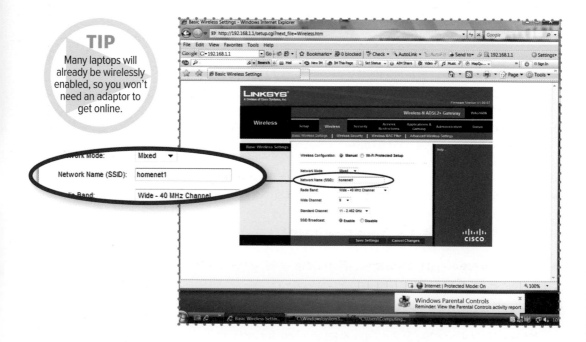

3 If you've secured your wireless network as suggested on page 78, you'll need to enter your encryption authorisation key when installing your adaptors

4 You can test your connection at this stage by opening your browser and trying to view a web page

Set up your workgroup

You'll need to set up a Windows Workgroup so that your PCs can talk to each other.

1 On one of your computers, click

2 Click **Control Panel**

3 Click **View network status and tasks** under the **Network Setup and Internet** heading

4 Click **Set up a new connection or network**

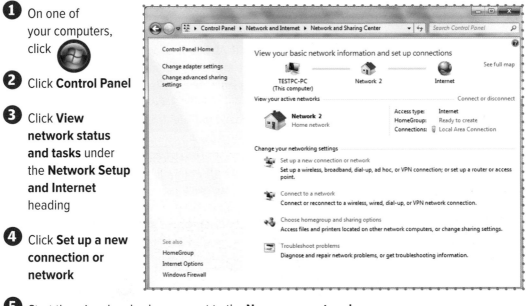

5 Start the wizard and, when you get to the **Name your network** page, type in something memorable instead of the default

6 Carry out the same steps for any other computers

7 Under **Properties**, on the **Computer Name** tab of the window that appears, click **Change** and enter a name for your PC

8 Enter the name of the workgroup you previously entered in the Network Setup Wizard

NEXT STEP ▶

Now you've set up your broadband connection, you'll want to get online (see page 73).

SWITCH BROADBAND PROVIDER

Before deciding to switch, you should talk to your current provider. If you switch broadband provider before the end of any minimum contract term, you may have to pay a hefty broadband cancellation fee. As long as you're outside your minimum contract period, however, your broadband provider will be keen to keep your custom and may well offer you a much more attractive deal meaning that you might not need to switch.

The process you use to switch internet suppliers will vary depending on whether you're just switching broadband, or whether you're changing your home phone service at the same time as your broadband.

Switch between ADSL broadband providers

If you are switching to and from ADSL broadband (broadband via a BT phone line), you'll need to use the MAC (migration authorisation code) process. MAC is a unique code that identifies a particular broadband line.

1 Ask your existing broadband provider for your broadband MAC. Make sure you stress you are only asking for your MAC and not cancelling your broadband account; some broadband providers will see requesting your MAC as a sign you want to cancel the service, which isn't great if you change your mind

2 Your broadband provider must provider a MAC on request and should send you the MAC within five working days. Your broadband MAC is valid for 30 days from the date it's issued

3 Give your MAC to the broadband internet provider you want to switch to. They should process your request and give you a transfer date

4 If you have problems switching between broadband providers because of difficulties obtaining a MAC from your existing broadband supplier, take a look at Ofcom's advice (www.ofcom.org.uk/complain/internet/switching/)

Switch to or from cable broadband

Cable broadband provider Virgin Media does not use the MAC broadband switching process. If you're switching your broadband service to or from Virgin Media, you simply cancel your existing broadband service and sign up to your new broadband service. You may need to have a new broadband line installed.

Switch your phone and broadband services simultaneously

If you're switching to or from a provider that offers phone and broadband services bundled together, you may not be able to use the MAC broadband switching process for technical reasons.

However, under Ofcom's switching regulations, phone and broadband bundle providers are still required to make the switch as easy for you as possible. You can find detailed advice on the various broadband and phone switching processes on Ofcom's website (www.ofcom.org.uk).

Each process aims for the minimum possible disruption, though there is a chance you may experience some loss of service. In each case, ask your new supplier which broadband and phone switching process to use and how long the switch will take.

⏵ Surfing the Web

YOUR WEB BROWSER

Your browser is your window on the web. It allows you to view and navigate between web pages. But there's a lot more your web browser can do too, such as storing your favourite web pages and protecting you from nasty surprises and common internet scams.

Windows 7 allows users to choose from several browsers including Microsoft's Internet Explorer (IE), Google Chrome, Mozilla Firefox and Apple Safari. When you use Windows for the first time, you will be asked to select which one to use as your default browser.

When you launch your web browser, the first thing you will see is a web page. This is known as your home page and each time you start your web surfing journey, you'll begin from here. The home page will have been already set by your choice of web browser, but it is very easy to change to something you prefer (see page 87).

Favorites
Clicking here will bring up a list of your saved favourite websites.

Main Internet Explorer Menu
Includes File, Edit, View, etc. Press the **Alt** key if the menu bar goes missing.

Address Bar
This is where you type the address of the web page you want to visit.

Multiple tabs
Tabs let you view different web pages without closing the first one. Click here to launch a new tab or press **Ctrl** + **T**. For more on tabbed browsing see page 89.

Toolbar
The row of buttons at the top of your browser, known as the toolbar, helps you travel through the web and keep track of where you've been.

Stop
Clicking here will stop a page loading.

Search box
This may be labelled Bing, Google or Yahoo! From here you can search for web pages using keywords.

Refresh
Clicking here shows any updates made to a web page during your visit. You can also use it if the page seems to have frozen before loading properly.

Home Page
The first page you see when your web browser launches.

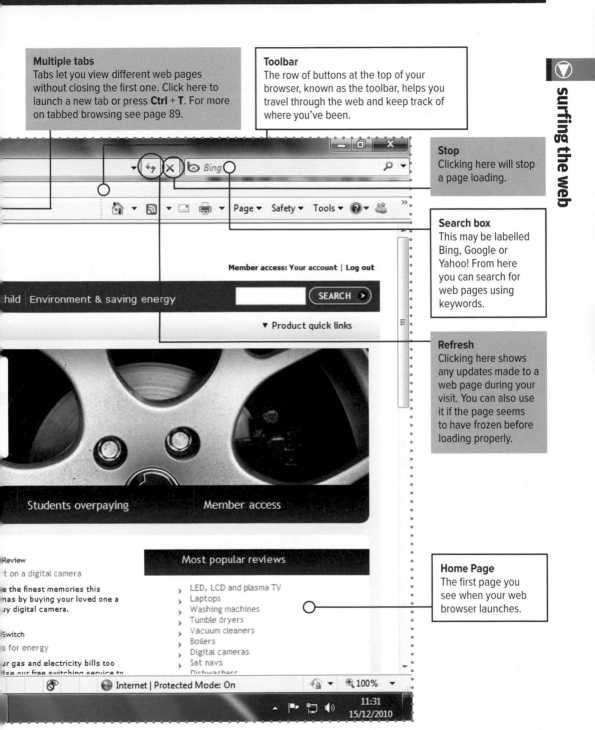

▶ Surfing the Web

INSTALLING A WEB BROWSER
To use the internet you need a web browser.

How to install a browser

 Visit the website of the web browser you wish to use, such as www.firefox.com

 Click **Download**

❸ Click **Run** and wait while the download completes. Click **Run** again

❹ Click **Yes** if you get a 'User Account Control' message

❺ Follow the onscreen instructions on the Setup Wizard (see left)

❻ Click **Next**

❼ Click **Next**, then **Install**

❽ Click **Finish**

Launch a browser

 To launch the web browser in Windows 7, click on in the bottom left of the screen

2 From the pop-up menu, click on **Internet**. The name of your browser will be listed underneath

3 A web browser window will appear in the centre of your screen. Now you can start surfing the internet

CHANGING YOUR DEFAULT BROWSER

There are a number of ways in which you can do this:

Download and install the new browser

When installed, open the new web browser that you wish to be your default program. A message will be displayed asking you if you want to make this web browser the default web browser. Click **Yes**.

Through the Start button

On the Windows desktop, click . Choose **Default Programs** on the list. You will be able to see a setting there for the default web browser that you want to choose. Set the default web browser and exit the screen.

In the browser itself

Open the web browser of your choice. Look for **Options** or **Settings** under the web browser **Preferences** to select it as the default.

▶ To make Internet Explorer 8 the default browser, open Internet Explorer and click on the **Tools** menu and then **Internet Options**. On the panel, click **Programs**. Make Internet Explorer the default browser and tick the **Tell me if Internet Explorer is not the default browser** box. Click **OK**

▶ In Firefox, for example, click on **Preferences** under the Firefox menu. In the box that appears, click on **Advanced** and **General** and then make sure that the box that says **Always check to see that Firefox is the default browser on start up** is ticked

⊙ Surfing the Web

ENTER A WEB ADDRESS

Every web page has its own web address, often referred to as the URL (Uniform Resource Locator). For example, the Which? website is www.which.co.uk. If you already know the web address for a page:

1 Type the full address into the address bar

2 Click the **Go** button or press **Enter**

NAVIGATE WEB PAGES

Back and forward buttons
As you move between web pages, Internet Explorer keeps track of the pages you've viewed. So, if you want to return to the last page you looked at, click the **Back** button. Continuing to click it more than once will go back a number of pages equal to the number of times you click it. Once you've clicked the **Back** button, you can also use the **Forward** button to return in the same manner.

Recent pages
Rather than repeatedly clicking the Back and Forward buttons, you can use the **Recent Pages** menu to revisit a page you've looked at recently. Click the arrow next to the Forward button and select a website from the list.

Refresh
Clicking this button reloads the current web page, which is useful if it appears to freeze while loading.

Home Page
Clicking this icon will take you to your home page – the first page you see when your web browser launches.

Favorites
Most browsers allow you to mark websites that you visit regularly as 'favourites' or 'bookmarks' so you can access them quickly rather than typing in an address for them each time you visit. In Internet Explorer 8, these sites are called Favorites and you can choose to list them horizontally on the menu bar. Clicking on the name of a favourite website will launch that particular site. Alternatively, you can save them in a list, which is accessed by clicking the **Favorites** button.

History
Your browser stores a history of all the websites you have visited, which is handy if you want to revisit a site you looked at earlier but if you can't quite remember the web address. However, this will take up space so you can delete this information to save space (or to protect your privacy) (see page 100).

TIP
To search for a specific word or phrase on a web page, press **Ctrl + F** and enter the word or phrase you want.

Links
Most web pages contain links to other pages. Links will often appear in a different colour, or as underlined text. To check whether something is a link, hover your cursor over it – if the mouse pointer turns into a pointing finger, it's a link and you can click on it. Click on a link and the relevant web page will open up.

Tabbed browsing
Tabbed browsing allows you to open multiple web pages at the same time within the same browser window. This can aid navigation by letting you open a link in a fresh tab (right click the link and select **Open in new tab**), while keeping the old page open as a reference.

You can switch between tabs by clicking on the one you want along the top edge of the main window. To close a tab, click on it to highlight it and then click the grey 'X'.

▶ Surfing the Web

TRY THIS

In addition to **Web** and **Images** (see page 92), Google also offers the search categories **News**, which searches for news-related stories, and **Shopping**, which looks for items for sale for whatever search term you've entered into the search box.

SEARCH THE WEB

If you want to look at a website but don't know the exact website address, you can search the internet using a search engine. You can also use it if you just want to find information on specific topic rather than a specific site.

The most popular search engine is Google (www.google.co.uk), but Yahoo (www.yahoo.com) and Microsoft's search engine (www.bing.com) are good alternatives. Simply type one of these addresses into the address bar to take you to its home page from where you can start your search.

Alternatively, the latest versions of web browsers Internet Explorer or Firefox have an instant search box located to the side of the address bar. You can type what you are looking for straight into this box and then press **Enter**.

1 Click once in the **Search** box in the top right-hand corner of the toolbar

2 Type what you're looking for and press **Enter**

3 Results will be displayed on screen

4 If you can't see what you're looking for, click **Next** at the bottom of the page to see more results. Or change the search terms to widen/tighten the search

SEARCH TIPS

▶ Using standard punctuation in your searches will make them more efficient. For instance, putting double quotes around a key phrase "John Smith" for example, restricts results to only those where the words appear together. Without the quotes a search would return results such as 'St John's, Smith Square'

▶ If you aren't sure whether a word has a hyphen in it or not, such as email or e-mail, keep the hyphen in; most search engines will check all variations

▶ Adding a + or – symbol will keep or remove certain words or phrases from search results. So, if you want to search for an Egyptian-themed hotel in Las Vegas, type Egypt + "Las Vegas" + hotel

▶ Searches won't include 'the', 'a', etc., so you don't need to include them in the search box

surfing the web

ADD ANOTHER SEARCH ENGINE BOX

You can use a different search engine, or add a specialist search engine box, for example, an eBay box, which will just search within the eBay site.

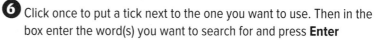

1 Click the arrow to the right of the magnifying glass icon and click **Find More Providers**

2 You'll see a list of options, including eBay

3 Click the one you want

4 Click **Add Provider**. Or follow the onscreen instructions to add one of your own that isn't in the list of options

5 When you want to switch to a different search engine box, click the arrow next to the magnifying glass to show the list

6 Click once to put a tick next to the one you want to use. Then in the box enter the word(s) you want to search for and press **Enter**

SEARCH FOR IMAGES AND FILES

Search engines automatically search for text results first, so if you want to search for images, then follow the relevant link or button (usually labelled 'Images') on your search engine's home page. Type in the key words relating to the image you're looking for (Albert Einstein, for example) and press **Enter**.

TRY THIS

You can restrict searches to certain websites. For example, you can look up a computer error code on Microsoft's website by putting the code you're searching for in the search box and following it with site:microsoft.com. The search engine will search results from Microsoft's website only.

You can also specify the types of documents you want to search for. For example you can narrow your search, so that your results only include PowerPoint presentations or PDF files – both popular file types. Follow the **Options** or **Advanced settings** links from your search engine's homepage. In Google, a quick way to search by file type is to include the word filetype: followed by the three-letter file extension of your desired file, followed by the key words. Here are some examples of what to type:

filetype:pdf – Searches PDF files
filetype:doc – Searches Word documents

Remember to include key words in the search query too (such as filetype:pdf BBC Annual Report).

Jargon buster

PDF
Portable Document Format, a file format created by Adobe that allows pages of text and graphics to be viewed and printed correctly on any computer.

▶ Surfing the Web

CHANGE YOUR HOME PAGE

Your home page is the first web page you see whenever you surf the internet. This is usually set to a default page, but can easily be changed.

1 Go to the web page you'd like to use as your home page

2 Click the arrow to the right of the **Home** button, and then click **Add or Change Home Page**

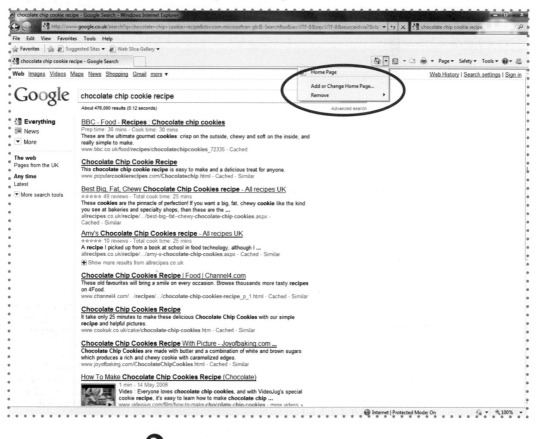

3 Click **Yes** to save your changes

If you change your mind, you can reset the homepage back to the default.
In Internet Explorer:

1 Click **Tools**, and then click **Internet Options**

2 Click the **General** tab

3 Click **Use default** to replace your current home page with the one
that was used when you first installed Internet Explorer

Internet Options   **?** **X**

| General | Security | Privacy | Content | Connections | Programs | Advanced |

Home page

To create home page tabs, type each address on its own line.

http://go.microsoft.com/fwlink/?LinkId=69157

Use current   Use default   Use blank

Browsing history

Delete temporary files, history, cookies, saved passwords,
and web form information.

☐ Delete browsing history on exit

Delete...   Settings

Search

Change search defaults.   Settings

Tabs

Change how webpages are displayed in   Settings
tabs.

Appearance

Colors   Languages   Fonts   Accessibility

OK   Cancel   Apply

4 Click **Apply** to save your changes

5 Click **OK**

TRY THIS

You don't have to type
http:// every time you
want to visit a website. If
you type everything after
the last forward slash,
Internet Explorer will fill
in the rest. For example,
just type www.bbc.co.uk
rather than http://www.
bbc.co.uk.

TRY THIS

If the web address you're
typing ends in .com, you
only need to type the
words between the
www. and .com and
press **Ctrl** + **ENTER**.
For example, type BBC in
the address bar and then
press **Ctrl** + **ENTER**.

Surfing the Web

BOOKMARK SITES

Web browsers allow you to bookmark your favourite websites so that you don't have to type the address into the address bar each time. In Internet Explorer they will be stored under Favorites and you will be able to click on the website's name to open the website quickly.

Add to your Favorites Bar

 Go to the website you want to add

2 Click the **Add to Favorites Bar** button on the toolbar

3 A button with the website name will appear on the Favorites Bar. To go to the site, simply click on the name

Add to your Favorites list

1 Go to the website you want to add

2 Click **Favorites**

3 Click **Add to Favorites** in the drop-down menu

4 In the box that appears, type a name for the website and click **Add**

Open a favourite web page in Internet Explorer

1 Click the **Favorites** button

2 Click the **Favorites** tab if it's not already selected

3 In the **Favorites** list, click the web page that you want to open

4 Or if you added a website to your Favorites Bar, you can click on it on the toolbar.

TIP
To delete a link or folder, right click on it, click **Delete**, then click **Yes**.

Manage your bookmarked sites

You can organise your favourite websites into separate folders, making them easier to find than if they are in one long list.

 In Internet Explorer, click the **Favorites** button and click the arrow next to **Add to Favorites**

2 Click **Organize Favorites**

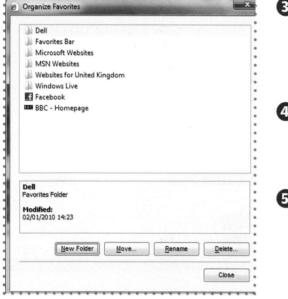

3 In the dialogue box that appears you'll see a list of your favourite links and folders

4 Click a folder to expand it and see the links it contains

5 To create a new folder, click **New Folder**. When a folder icon appears, right click on it

TRY THIS

Click a link or folder and simply drag it to the new position or folder. You can also move items by right-clicking the link or folder, clicking **Move**, and then choosing the folder you want to move it to.

6 Click **Rename** and type a name for it (for example, Holiday websites) and press **Enter**

7 When you've finished, click **Close**

surfing the web

⏵ Surfing the Web

MAKE WEB PAGES MORE READABLE

Internet Explorer 8 has several accessibility options to help increase the readability of web pages.

Change web page text size

1 In Internet Explorer, click the **Page** button, then click **Text Size**

2 Click the size you want

Make web pages bigger

Internet Explorer Zoom lets you enlarge or reduce the view of a web page. Unlike changing font size, zoom enlarges or reduces everything on the page, including text and images. You can zoom from 10% to 1,000%.

1 On the bottom right of the Internet Explorer screen, click the arrow next to the **Change Zoom Level** button

2 To go to a pre-defined zoom level, click the percentage of enlargement or reduction you want. Holding down the button will cycle through 100%, 125%, and 150%, giving you a quick enlargement of the web page

③ Or, to specify a level, click **Custom**. In the **Percentage zoom** box, type a zoom value, and then click **OK**

④ If you have a mouse with a wheel, hover your cursor over the page, hold down the **CTRL** key, and then scroll the wheel to zoom in or out (up for in and down for out)

⑤ From the keyboard you can increase or decrease the zoom value in 1% increments. To zoom in, press **CTRL + PLUS SIGN** (+). To zoom out, press **CTRL + MINUS SIGN** (-). To restore the zoom to 100%, press **CTRL + 0**

Change web page colours

You can change a website's foreground and background colours as well as the colour of the links (as well as changing the font type and size). These are all useful if you have low vision, or need larger fonts or high-contrast colours for great legibility.

① In Internet Explorer, click the **Tools** button, and then click **Internet Options**

② To change the font, click the **General** tab, and then click **Fonts**

③ Specify the fonts you want to use, and then click **OK**

④ To change the colours, click the **General** tab, and then click **Colors**

⑤ Clear the **Use Windows Colors** check box, and then select the colours you want to use

⑥ When you've finished, click **OK** and then **OK** again

Colors	☒

☐ Use **h**over color

Colors

☐ Use **W**indows colors

Text: ▮

Background: ▭

V**i**sited: ▮

U**n**visited: ▮

H**o**ver: ▭

How to ignore preset colors

| OK | Cancel |

INTERNET EXPLORER TIPS

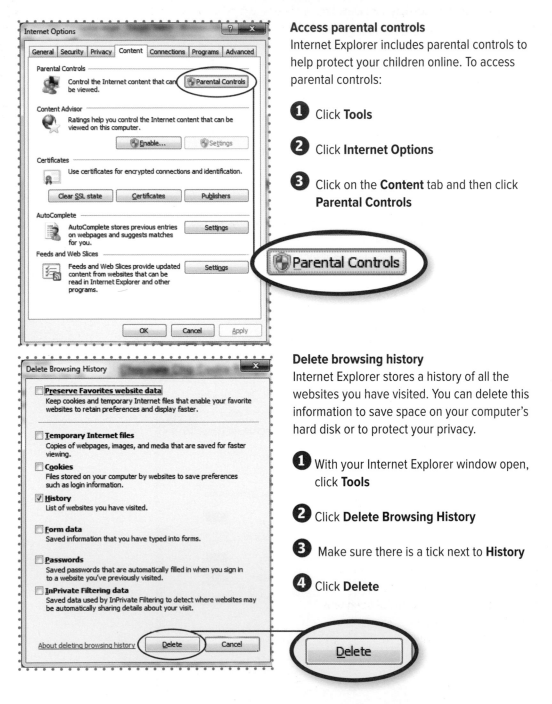

Access parental controls

Internet Explorer includes parental controls to help protect your children online. To access parental controls:

1 Click **Tools**

2 Click **Internet Options**

3 Click on the **Content** tab and then click **Parental Controls**

Delete browsing history

Internet Explorer stores a history of all the websites you have visited. You can delete this information to save space on your computer's hard disk or to protect your privacy.

1 With your Internet Explorer window open, click **Tools**

2 Click **Delete Browsing History**

3 Make sure there is a tick next to **History**

4 Click **Delete**

General internet shortcuts

▶ Flick back and forward between web pages you've visited by pressing the **Shift** key and using the scroll wheel on the top of your mouse (up is forward, down is backward on the scroll wheel)

▶ Change the size of the text on a web page by clicking **View** and then **Text Size**. You can then select from Largest to Smallest

▶ Press **Ctrl + F** to search for a specific word or phrase on a web page you're visiting and enter the word or phrase

These may be useful to save having to click on a number of buttons.

F11	Turns Full Screen Mode on or off (removing the toolbar and taskbar, or reinstating them)
TAB	Moves the cursor through the Address Bar, Refresh button, Search Box etc until you reach the item you want
Ctrl + F	Finds a word or phrase on a web page
Ctrl + N	Opens the current web page in a new window
Ctrl + P	Prints the page
Ctrl + A	Selects all items on the page
Ctrl + PLUS SIGN	Zooms in
Ctrl + MINUS SIGN	Zooms out
Ctrl + 0	Zooms to 100 per cent

Internet navigation shortcuts

Alt + HOME	Goes to the home page
Alt + LEFT	Goes back a page
Alt + RIGHT	Goes forward a page
F5	Refreshes a page
ESC	Stops downloading a page

Tab shortcuts (see page 89)

Ctrl + Q	Opens Quick Tab view
Ctrl + T	Opens a new tab
Ctrl + SHIFT + Q	Shows list of open tabs
Ctrl + TAB	Switches to next tab
Ctrl + SHIFT + TAB	Switches to previous tab

▶ Online Activities

CREATE AN EBAY ACCOUNT

eBay is a website that allows you to buy and sell items – the online equivalent of the classified pages of your newspaper. Before you can start advertising your items or buying others, however, you'll need an eBay account.

1 Go to the eBay home page at www.ebay.co.uk

2 Click on **Register**

3 Enter your name, address and email address

4 Choose a username

BID ON EBAY

An eBay auction works on the same principle as an auction in an auction house – the highest bidder wins, but in this case the auction takes place over a number of days and has a cut-off date and time.

1 Find the item that you want to bid on and click on it

2 Enter the amount you want to bid and click on **Place Bid**

3 Ensure your bid is higher than the current one then click **Confirm Bid** (note that, by doing so, you agree to buy the item if you are successful)

Alternatively, you can enter the maximum you are prepared to pay for the item and eBay's proxy bidding service will automatically bid incrementally on your behalf up to that amount. If your bid is the highest at the cut-off time, then you've won the auction.

If your bid is successful, you'll be told by email. It will contain details of the types of payment the seller accepts: credit or debit card or PayPal, for example. eBay's preferred method is the electronic payment system, PayPal, which it owns. PayPal transfers funds between buyers and sellers without them having to exchange bank account details (see page 106).

BE CAREFUL

Some sellers may ask you to pay via money transfer service Western Union. Don't! eBay has banned the use of these transactions on the website because money transfers leave no electronic paper trail or proof of payment and can leave you out of pocket with nothing to show for your money.

SELL ON EBAY

To sell an item on eBay, you'll need to log on to the website and press the **Sell** button. Then you need to follow the onscreen instructions to fill in the details of your item. The better you do this, the more money someone is likely to bid.

Here are a few simple tips you can use to make your auction stand out from the crowd.

TRY THIS

eBay also has a great community of users who discuss their top selling tips on the eBay's online forums. Check out your favourite sales categories at http://groups.ebay.co.uk or ask other members for advice at http://pages.ebay.co.uk/community/answercenter.

▶ One of the first decisions you'll need to make is in which category to list your item. If you're unsure, type in a few key words about it and eBay will suggest a category for you. It's possible to list products in multiple categories to give them more exposure – but your listing fees will be doubled as a result (for more on these fees see Costs, opposite)

▶ Each eBay listing has a one-line title and you'll need to choose a catchy title to grab people's attention. Buyers will typically conduct title searches and results will be listed according to relevance. The more information you provide, the more chance there is that potential buyers will click through to your item

▶ It's essential that you include a photograph of your item. Buyers want to be able to see what they're buying and it gives them a good indication of its condition. The first photograph is free, additional ones will cost more. Make sure your pictures are clear and well lit

▶ Keep descriptions (including the title) up front and honest, while remaining positive and upbeat about the item

▶ Remember to get the brand/model names and spelling variations correct

▶ Don't forget to list all postage information and returns policies clearly. For example, if you're willing to post your item overseas, you can quote a separate postage cost for this

▶ Make sure your listing ends when traffic to eBay is busiest as it'll attract last-minute bids. Weekends and weekday evenings usually attract the most buyers

▶ Research how much items have sold for in the past by browsing 'completed items' and learn from other sellers' successful listings

▶ Start your bidding at a low price – it will attract more people to place a bid (you can choose what price to start your item at when you first list it)

▶ Always respond to bidders' enquiries in a timely manner

▶ Build up a reputation selling smaller value items. The higher your feedback rating, the more people are likely to trust you (see page 107)

Costs

You'll have to pay to list your item on eBay just as you'd pay for a classified advertisement in a newspaper. eBay charges two types of fee: listing fees (the cost to insert your item; this depends on its starting price) and final value fees (a commission based on the price your item sells for). See http://pages.ebay.co.uk/help/sell/fees.html for details of all the latest prices.

Postage and packaging

Post and packaging prices are paid for by the buyer, but as a seller you need to list these charges upfront. To work out what these will be, you will need to weigh your item along with all your packaging and make sure you've measured the package's exact dimensions. Then consult the Royal Mail website (www.royalmail.com) to determine your shipping charges – these will differ depending on the level of postage you are offering (1st or 2nd class or Special Delivery, say).

It's more environmentally conscious to recycle packaging, so you can make your sales more attractive by passing on these cost savings, or even offering postage and packaging for free as an incentive for buyers to bid on your item.

You can also offer post and packaging prices for those bidding in other countries (this is optional). If you want to do this, remember to add alternative postal charges in the relevant section when listing your item.

BE CAREFUL

eBay allows buyers to leave you feedback, which is added to your feedback rating. It's important to ensure that you have a good rating as buyers often check this before choosing to bid in an auction.

USE PAYPAL

Unless you're selling a car or property, to sell on eBay you are required to offer PayPal as a method of payment (www.paypal.co.uk). It gives you a secure online account that stores your credit card or bank account details, but won't reveal these details to the person you're buying from or selling to (for more on eBay, see page 103).

The majority of eBay transactions are with PayPal. Each listing will say whether the item is eligible for buyer protection; most tangible items are. PayPal is also fast and free for buyers. As a seller you'll be charged a small transaction fee. After eBay's taken its cut, your received funds are transferred into your PayPal account, from where you can withdraw it into your bank account or credit it to your card. To set up a PayPal account:

BE CAREFUL

Watch out for scam emails claiming to be from PayPal and asking for your account details. Always go directly to your PayPal account via the website – don't click on any links within emails.

1 Go to www.paypal.com

2 Click **Sign up**

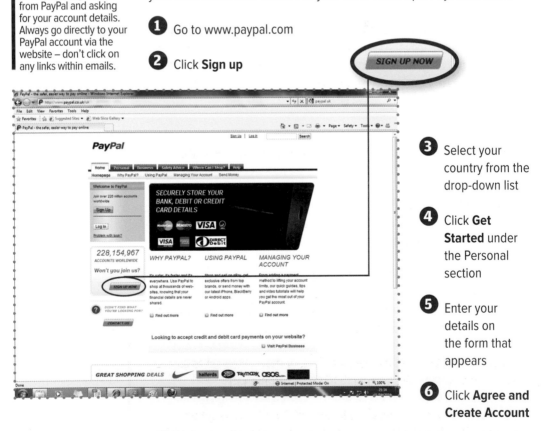

3 Select your country from the drop-down list

4 Click **Get Started** under the Personal section

5 Enter your details on the form that appears

6 Click **Agree and Create Account**

7 You can now log into your account and manage your transactions

EBAY FEEDBACK RATINGS

Buyers are asked to rate sellers out of five on several criteria. During the auction, you may receive questions from potential bidders via the eBay site, perhaps on the exact condition of an item on offer, how old it is and what it originally cost. Making sure that you respond quickly increases your chance of a sale and will help to boost a potential buyer's confidence in you. The areas you'll be rated on are item as described, communication, dispatch time and postage and packaging charges.

YOUR RIGHTS ON EBAY

Since eBay only facilitates transactions, it is not responsible for them. If you're having problems with something you've bought, your first port of call is to contact the seller via the website.

However, eBay does have a system set up to deal with any disputes. If you don't receive the item or if it isn't as described, you're protected for the full amount so long as you file a dispute with eBay within 45 days and you paid for the item all in one go. The listing will say whether the item is eligible for buyer protection.

TIPS FOR SHOPPING SAFELY ONLINE

Regardless of which sites you shop at online, do make sure you take some safety steps before you go ahead.

Important safety steps

▶ Before you buy, ensure you have a firewall switched on and anti-virus and anti-spyware software installed (see page 200)

▶ Choose a reputable retailer, such as a familiar high-street store, or use an online directory such as www.safebuy.org.uk or www.shopsafe. co.uk that lists only shops offering secure credit card transactions, with obvious delivery prices and clear returns policies

▶ Secure web addresses start with the letters **https**, instead of **http**, and you should see a padlock symbol at the top of the page

▶ Find out how easy the website is to contact. Look for links called **Contact us** or **Help** to find the physical address and phone number. Call to make sure the line is working and that someone picks up. If there's only an email address, send one to see how quickly they reply

▶ Online Activities

TRY THIS
You can use price comparison websites to find out where to buy items for the cheapest price. Popular sites include PriceRunner (www.pricerunner.co.uk) and Kelkoo (www.kelkoo.co.uk).

Buy an item

Once you've spent some time browsing and have decided what to buy, it's time to go to the checkout:

1 Click the button marked **Add to shopping basket**

2 Many websites allow you to **View basket** so you can check what you've added, the total cost, and how many of each item you've ordered. Then you can either shop some more or make your payment

3 To pay, click the **Proceed to checkout** button (or equivalent). Be aware that many online retailers will only deliver goods to the billing address of your credit card. If you haven't already registered, you'll be asked to

4 While you're registering, investigate the small print/terms and conditions. How much does delivery cost? Are goods in stock? Can you send items back if they're not what you expected?

5 If you're happy, enter your card details, including the start and expiry date. Many websites now ask for the security code to ensure the person ordering has the card in front of them. This is on the signature strip on the back of your credit card; just enter the last 3 digits

6 Ensure you keep a record of the transaction and the order number. You should receive a receipt via email; if you have spam-filtering software, this email may end up in your junk folder so do check it

Internet payments

If you use a credit card to pay for goods worth more than £100 (and up to £30,000), your card company is jointly liable with the company that you buy from for any problems. For smaller purchases, an e-cash system such as PayPal is often used. These systems allow you to send or receive payments securely over the web without sharing your financial details or credit card number with anyone else.

Know your rights

Shopping online can be more convenient and cheaper than the high street, but it can be easy to make a mistake when ordering online shopping, and sometimes what you receive isn't what you expected. So what are your rights as a shopper?

If you buy online from a UK or EU-based retailer, you have the same rights as if you'd bought from a shop. Under the Sale of Goods Act, items purchased must be of satisfactory quality, fit for purpose and as described when sold. If a retailer breaches any of these terms, you have the right to reject the goods within a reasonable time and get a full refund. Or you can demand that the retailer repairs or replaces the item. If you send goods back for any reason that is the fault of the supplier, you should not have to pay the postage.

Under the E-Commerce Regulations, online shops must set out the stages you have to complete to place an order. You must also be given the chance to check your details before placing the order. If the online shop confirms acceptance of your order, you have a legally binding contract, but if it simply acknowledges your order, you don't.

The E-Commerce Regulations also state that the online shop has to give details of who they are and provide a geographical address and an email address at which to contact them. The online shop's terms and conditions should say who pays for returning goods. If they don't, they have to pay.

Pay close attention to an online store's terms and conditions before you purchase. An example of an online shop's terms and conditions to watch out for is when they say that the price of your order will be fixed the day the goods are dispatched to you. This can mean that they may charge a higher price than when you placed the order, but they must still give your right to cancel under the Distance Selling Regulations (see below).

Cooling-off period

If you change your mind about the goods, or they don't arrive on time, the Distance Selling Regulations (DSR) give you a cooling-off period. This starts from the moment you place the order and ends seven working days from the day after you receive the goods. During this period you can cancel without having to give a reason. Contact the seller and quote the DSR to get a refund and arrange to send back the purchase. These regulations don't apply to items bought from foreign websites or to items such as unsealed CDs/DVDs, perishable items, such as food and flowers, and personalised goods.

▶ Online Activities

WATCH TELEVISION ONLINE

With a fast broadband connection (at least 2Mbps) you can watch TV programmes on your PC over the internet. The most popular service is iPlayer from the BBC, which lets you catch up on virtually all BBC TV shows that have been broadcast in the past seven days.

You can either watch these shows in a lower-quality 'streaming' mode directly on the iPlayer website or you can download crisper, full-length shows to your computer. If you use the download method, you'll have 30 days to start watching them (see page 112) – and you won't have to be connected to the internet.

(see page 112)

Check your internet usage allowances

First check with your ISP about your monthly internet usage allowances, which are calculated by the amount of data you download from the internet. If you exceed your allowance, you may be charged extra or your broadband speed may be temporarily reduced. Downloading an hour-long programme will use up around 600MB of your monthly allowance.

Browse for a programme

1 Go to the iPlayer website (www.bbc.co.uk/iplayer). The week's TV highlights are listed in panels at the top of the home page

TRY THIS

Other TV channels, including ITV, Channel 4, Five and Sky, offer their own online TV viewing options. Search for and visit the website of each TV channel for viewing information.

2 Click on **TV Channels** to browse by channel. Or click on **Categories** to search through categories that include Drama, Music, News and Children's

3 Alternatively, you can type in the programme name in the **Search** box at the top of the page. Titles that fit the search will automatically drop down beneath the box. Choose the programme and episode you want, and click on the link to visit the show's page

View a programme directly from the website

1 When you choose a programme, a large **Play** icon will show in the middle of the screen. It will automatically start streaming to your computer

2 To view in full-screen mode, click the square icon at the bottom right of the viewing screen. To exit full-screen mode, press the **ESC** key

3 To increase or decrease the volume, click on the volume icon and move the pop-up slider up or down to suit

Monitor your progress

If you get any problems with interruptions or pauses during viewing, check the progress indicator underneath the viewing screen. The white bar shows how much of the show has been made ready (or 'buffered') for viewing. The pink bar shows how much of the show you've watched. For you to watch the show smoothly, the white bar always has to be ahead of the pink one, so you may need to pause the show until the white bar progresses far enough. If it doesn't, your broadband connection may be busy and you'll need to try again later.

online activities

Jargon buster ▶

Streaming
Programmes that are sent in compressed form over the internet and shown on the viewer in real time.

▶ Online Activities

Downloading shows for viewing

1 Choose your programme as above. Instead of clicking the Play icon, click **Download** underneath the viewing screen

 2 The first time you do this, you'll be prompted to install the iPlayer Download Manager software. Click **Save** to acquire the installation file and double click on the file to install the software. Follow the setup steps as prompted

3 Once installed, you'll return to the iPlayer website. This time when you click the **Download** link your show will start downloading via the iPlayer software. Progress is indicated on the iPlayer Download Manager screen

View the downloaded show

Once your show is downloaded it will be stored on your computer for 30 days. However, after you click on it to view the first time, you will have just seven days to watch it before it is deleted.

1 Find your show's listing on your computer by launching BBC iPlayer Desktop from the **Start** menu

2 Once BBC iPlayer Desktop appears, click the **Downloads** tab to see a list of downloaded programmes. Click **Watch Now** to view any programme listed

3 As with streaming, you can view shows in full screen mode by clicking the square icon at the bottom right of the viewing screen. Press the **ESC** button to exit this mode

WATCH A YOUTUBE CLIP

YouTube (www.youtube.com) is a video-sharing website that lets you search for and view video clips added by members.

You can search on the site and watch clips without logging in, but, by creating an account, you can add comments about video clips that you have viewed, bookmark your favourites and give them star ratings out of five. You can even post your own creations to the site.

Search for a clip

1 Type www.youtube.com into the address bar of your web browser

TRY THIS

Can't hear any sound with the clip you are watching? Your computer's sound might be turned down or muted – check the volume by clicking on the speaker icon in the system tray (bottom right of your screen) (see page 11).

2 Whenever a video is posted to YouTube, its author assigns search terms (key words) to it that help other people find it. Type a few key words in the search box that describe what you're looking for. If you want to look at some videos of koalas, for example, try cute koalas

3 Click **Search**

Jargon buster

System tray
An area on your Windows desktop that displays icons accompanying programs, and alerts you to their status.

Online Activities

4 You'll be shown a list of results that match your search

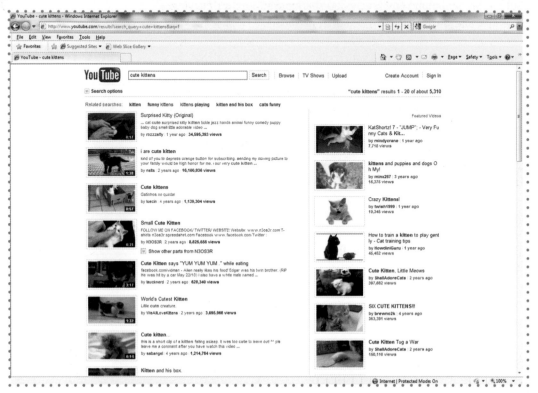

5 To watch a video clip, click on a video link and it should start playing automatically

6 Click the **Pause** symbol to pause the clip and the **Play** symbol to resume play. Adjust volume using the slider bar

 NEXT STEP

Once you've set up a YouTube account you can post your own videos by clicking on the **Upload** button in the top right of the screen and following the onscreen instructions.

7 To blow up the clip so it can be viewed larger in full screen mode, click the button at the bottom right corner of the video. Press **Esc** to return to small screen mode

8 Rather than search for a specific clip, you can also browse what's popular. Click the **Most Popular** tab on the home page and choose a subject on the left, such as Sport

9 Under **Most Viewed** you can see what video clips have been the most popular that day

SOCIAL NETWORKING EXPLAINED

The internet has changed the way we connect to friends and family and meet new people. Removing the need for face-to-face contact or for picking up a telephone, we can now get in touch instantly with others anywhere in the world.

At the heart of this change are social networks – websites that let you chat and interact with others online. Some people use them to keep in touch with friends and family, others to meet new friends with shared interests, hobbies or causes. There are hundreds of different social networking sites. Some sites are tailored for more specific users while larger, general sites, such as Facebook, Twitter and MySpace, attract millions of users.

Your profile

Most social network sites give you the chance to create a profile page, where you can tell others about yourself. You'll be asked for basic information such as your age and gender, and you can add details about your hobbies and interests, likes and dislikes so that others can see if they have anything in common with you.

Social networks offer several ways to interact with others. You can send personal emails, you can leave messages or pictures on friends' message boards or join a group of people with a shared interest – say specific types of movies or Greenpeace. You can share photos and video clips with your friends, and even play games like chess or Scrabble with them online.

Who uses social networks?

People of all ages now use social networking sites. Your initial contact on the site is likely to be with friends and family; people with whom you already have something in common. Once you're established on a site you may wish to make friends with new people – perhaps those with whom you share an interest or who live in your area.

Which social network site should I join?

If you happen to know that loads of your friends are already using a particular service, that alone might be enough to make you sign up. But if you're joining to meet new people, or to find people with common interests, you might want to look for a site that's targeted at a particular demographic. For example Saga Zone (www.sagazone.co.uk) is aimed at people over fifty.

Access and join a social network site

You access a social network site via your web browser in the same way as you would visit any website. You don't need any specialist software to use these sites, although some of them will encourage you to download new applications or browser plug-ins.

1 Go to the home page of the social networking site you want to join, say Facebook

2 Click on **Sign Up** or **Register** (this will differ depending on the site)

3 You'll need to enter some personal details to get started. The type of information you're required to give varies from website to website

4 Once you've filled in your details, a confirmation email is usually sent to your email address. You must click on the link provided in this email to activate your account

5 You can now log in to your account to begin finding friends and adding information to your profile

Find friends

A friend may invite you to join a social networking group to which they already belong, in which case they've already found you. You can search for a friend by manually entering their name into a Search box on the site. Alternatively, some social networking websites will search their sites for people listed in your email address book and let you know if they are members of the site.

Security

When you put personal details on the internet, you must consider where they will end up. If things go wrong (the site you're signed up with has a security breach, for example), your information could end up in the wrong hands. The social networking sites work hard to prevent this.

BE CAREFUL

Most social networking sites enable you to choose whether your profile is public or private (look for Privacy settings or a similar title). This affects who can view your profile and send you messages.

▶ Online Activities

POPULAR SOCIAL NETWORKING SITES

Sagazone – www.sagazone.co.uk

This is a social network site run by Saga Group and aimed at the over-50s market. The site lacks many of the advanced features found on sites like Facebook, but its carefully chosen demographic means it attracts a large number of like-minded people. Signing up is a little convoluted but, overall, the interface is simple and well signposted.

Facebook – www.facebook.com

Facebook's popularity continues to grow worldwide. It's a site designed to help you find and keep in touch with friends. It is easy to navigate through the busy site and, once connected, to see what friends are doing. It offers various privacy settings on the site to protect users' information.

Flickr – www.flickr.com

Flickr is a photo-sharing website (see page 160) that has established a strong following among those keen to show off their photography skills. Free account holders can upload 100MB of photos to share, and can join in discussion groups and send messages to other users. It lacks sophisticated features, but is easy to use and allows you to restrict who can see your information.

Friends Reunited – www.friendsreunited.co.uk

Started in 1999 to help people track down old school friends, Friends Reunited has over 18 million users and has expanded to include school-based discussion groups and the additional ability to search by workplace, clubs and even the armed forces. The site used to charge for sending messages but now it's free. There aren't many fancy social networking features or advanced privacy features here. Once your profile is up, anyone can see it, but email addresses aren't revealed without your permission.

Twitter – www.twitter.com

This is a site that allows its users to send and read text-based messages of up to 140 characters. These messages, known as tweets, are displayed on your profile page and delivered to your friends who are known as 'followers'. You can restrict delivery to certain people or, by default, allow open access.

Yahoo! Groups – http://groups.yahoo.com

Yahoo! Groups lacks many of the features people often associate with social networking groups. However, it lets you join or set up discussion groups on a range of topics. You need to register for a Yahoo! account first by visiting www.yahoo.co.uk and clicking on Sign Up. While you can't customise your profile and add features in the way you can on more sophisticated sites, Yahoo! Groups is an excellent starting point for anyone who's interested in trying out social networking for the first time.

TRY THIS

Comment on today's consumer issues and discuss how they affect your life on the Which? Conversation site: http://conversation.which.co.uk/.

SET UP A FACEBOOK ACCOUNT

Facebook is one of the biggest and most popular social networking sites and is a great way to keep in touch with friends and family.

TRY THIS

The right-hand side of your Facebook home page is the Highlights panel – a digest of photos, events and notes that the site thinks will interest you, based on your interests, posts and what your friends have been up to.

1 To join Facebook, type www.facebook.com into the address bar of your web browser. Once the page is loaded, you need to register – this means choosing a username and entering a valid email address. You'll need these each time you log in

2 Complete your Facebook registration by clicking on the link sent by Facebook to your email. You will be asked to fill out your Profile information and to upload a photo or take one with your webcam. You can skip both these stages if you wish

3 Facebook will invite you to locate friends on the site by entering your webmail address and password. It will then search your webmail for names that appear in its own database and, if found, will then show their account details. Most of the popular webmail services can be searched, including Gmail, Hotmail and AOL

4 The Find Friends feature lets you locate people with the email application you use, such as Outlook Express or Apple Mail. Click on **Find more friends** on the right-hand side of the screen. Enter your email address and password and click **Enter**. Alternatively, you can click **Friends** underneath your profile picture and follow the instructions under **Add personal contacts as friends**

5 On Facebook, friends need to be confirmed by both people before they become 'official', and appear on your friends list

FACEBOOK TIPS

Edit your profile

1 Your Facebook profile shows who you are, with sections including Personal Information and Contact Information. Though there is no obligation to do so, filling these in will make it easier for other people to find you on Facebook. Click **Profile** in the menu bar and then the **Edit Profile** link

2 Adding a profile picture makes it easier for friends to identify you as the real you, especially if you have a common name. To add a profile picture, click on **Profile** in the **Menu** bar. Click on your profile picture, then click **Change Profile picture**. You can then browse for a picture on your computer in the normal way (see page 156)

Write something

1 You can publish your status, photos, notes and more using the 'publisher' feature. This comes in the form of a text box at the top of your page, below your name, just above the 'stream' of information

2 Once you've added content, click **Share** to publish it to Facebook. Your posts show up both on your Wall and on your friends' home pages so they can keep up to date with what you're doing

3 You have two streams. One is your Wall, which is in your profile area (click **Profile**) and the other is the News Feed on your home page (what you see when you first log in). The News Feed shows you posts from your friends. The Wall is a space on each user's profile page that lets friends post messages (these can be seen by other friends)

⊳ Online Activities

SOCIAL NETWORKING ETIQUETTE

Your social life online will require some management and, as in the real world, the rules of social etiquette apply when dealing with other people. Here are some top tips for getting it right:

▶ Keep personal life and professional life separate. Use a business-focused networking site such as LinkedIn for co-workers, and maintain a Facebook account for your family and friends. If you only have a Facebook account, give different access settings to colleagues and family. Click **Settings** in the upper-right corner of your Facebook profile page, and select **Privacy Settings**. Then select **Profile**. In the **Basic** tab, you can set various privacy settings, such as deciding who can see a photo album and messages posted by friends

▶ Remember that you're dealing with a public space. Make sure that all your blogs, comments and photos are those you would be happy for anyone to see. And, remember, once posted, you can't take them back

▶ Don't bombard people with friend requests without a personal message

▶ Accumulating a huge number of 'friends' is common on social networking sites, mainly because it is so easy to make new connections even with complete strangers. However, a good rule of thumb is that you should invite only people that you have some kind of link to, even if they are a friend of a friend of a friend

▶ If you accept friends from several generations, such as your children and grandchildren, be aware of the type of content you and your other adult friends post. Consider if it is suitable for younger friends to see or be aware of

▶ People know that, when they send an invite, you have the right to accept or reject their invitations. In real life it might be considered rude, but online etiquette allows you either to reply with a 'No, thank you' or not to reply at all

▶ Don't post unfriendly comments about people or use your blog for a personal crusade against anyone

Jargon buster ⊳

Blog
A regularly updated online journal.

▶ On Facebook, don't tag friends in pictures that might harm their reputation or cost them their jobs

▶ Don't share private conversations on your Facebook wall or to the entire Twitter audience

▶ Don't spam people – by constantly asking them to watch and rate your video on YouTube, for example (see page 113). Avoid repeatedly inviting disinterested friends on Facebook to play online games or try new software applications

▶ While social networking sites are for sharing interests with other like-minded people, be careful of links. Some have links to adult websites, illegal downloads or harmful viruses

▶ Online Activities

SET UP AN ONLINE BANK ACCOUNT

You can set up an online account using your existing bank account, or open a brand new internet-only account.

Your own bank

1 Type the address of your bank's website into the address bar. You'll find the website address on your bank statement or other literature your bank may have sent you

2 On the bank's home page click on **Register** (or similar – what you need to click on will vary depending on your bank)

3 To access your existing bank account online, you'll need your sort code and account number to hand. Type them in when prompted, along with your personal details (likely to include your name, address and date of birth). You may also need a User ID or specific login details – contact your bank to check

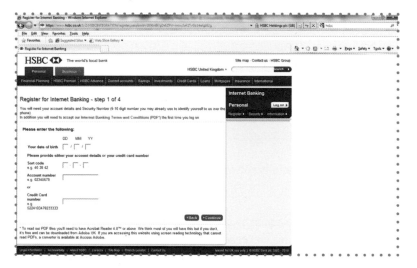

 4 Once your account is set up, and if you're sure that your PC and internet connection are secure (see page 198), you can now log on to your account. If you lose or forget your password, you should phone your bank

 5 Always remember to log out of your account when you're finished

A new online bank account with another bank

1 If you want to set up a brand new account online, enter that bank's website address in the address bar and go to the current account section where you can click on your desired account and fill in the form that appears

2 You'll usually get a decision on whether your application has been successful within a couple of minutes

3 As above, ensure that your PC and internet connection are secure before logging on to your account

TRY THIS

Many banks offer free security software or a subscription for a certain period when you sign up. Always check the terms and conditions before you subscribe to anything. It's important to make sure you have anti-virus and anti-spyware installed on your computer, and that your firewall is switched on. Make sure you run regular virus and spyware scans. For more on securing your computer, see page 198.

BE CAREFUL

Fraudsters frequently rely on people using poorly chosen passwords such as 'password' or a sequence of letters or repeated numbers. To make sure you have a strong password, use a mixture of numbers and upper and lower case letters, and don't use the same one that you use for other accounts, like your email, for example.

BANK ACCOUNT SAFETY TIPS

▶ Only log on to your online bank account if you know you're using a secure PC. Avoid using public computers, including those in your office, as you can't be sure of how secure they are

▶ Secure sites will be prefixed with https:// (rather than http://) and a padlock will appear by the website address

▶ If possible, memorise your password rather than writing it down. Don't give your password to anyone, and never give your full password over the phone or email. Your bank will never ask for your whole password, they will only ask for certain digits, for example, the first and fourth numbers in your password, so beware of anyone who does

Jargon buster

Phishing
A type of email scam where you're tricked into giving away personal details on a spoof website that resembles the site of an official organisation (a bank, for example).

▶ Make sure your security software is up to date, and secure your wireless network

▶ Only access your account by using the website address provided by the bank. This means you can be certain that you are on the correct (safe and secure) website when you enter your details. If you search for your bank's site using a search engine (like Google or Yahoo!, for example), you could end up on a site set up by fraudsters to illegally obtain your bank details

▶ Never follow a link from an email claiming to be from your bank

COMMUNICATING

By reading this chapter you will get to grips with:

 Sending emails

 Dealing with spam

 Chatting online using a webcam

⏵ Email

EMAIL

An email account allows you to send and receive messages. You can also store emails that you want to keep and create an address book with important information like phone numbers and addresses, as well as email addresses. To send emails, you can either use an email client like Windows Live Mail (see page 135), or a webmail account like Hotmail or Gmail (see pages 130 and 132).

Email clients refer simply to the email programs where emails are stored on your computer. Many email activities (reading received messages, composing messages, etc.) can be carried out when you're not online, but to send and receive emails you need to be connected to the internet. Webmail accounts can only be accessed when you're connected to the internet, but the benefit is that you can access your email easily from any computer with the internet, not just your home computer.

CHOOSING A WEBMAIL ACCOUNT

There are four major webmail providers: AOL Mail, GMail, Windows Live Hotmail and Yahoo! Mail. The number of emails you can store in each varies. Yahoo! offers unlimited storage, while other webmail accounts tend to offer around 5GB of storage – more than enough for the average user. You also need to be aware that if you don't use your webmail for a number of months, the service provider might switch off or deactivate the account.

As well as email, some webmail accounts also offer features such as office software, photo tools and instant chat.

CREATE A HOTMAIL ACCOUNT

The first thing you'll need to do is set up a Windows Live ID, which will give you access to a personalised home page as well as a Windows Live Mail account.

 Type http://home.live.com into your web browser's address bar

 Click on the **Sign up** button

3 Enter the email address you would like and click **Check availability**. If your preferred name isn't available, Windows Live will suggest alternatives. For example, if JohnSmith isn't available, you may be offered JohnSmith342

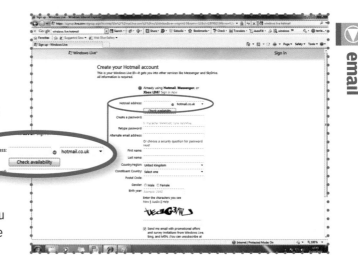

4 Choose a password for your account. Either then enter an alternative email address (if you have one) so that Windows Live Mail can send you a reminder of your password if needed, or click **Or choose a security question for password reset**. Click the drop-down arrow and choose a reminder question

5 Enter your personal details and copy the series of characters at the bottom of the screen. Click **I accept**

6 To make changes to your profile (this contains information such as contact information), click **Profile** then click **Edit Profile**

7 Click the **Edit** buttons to add a picture, enter your age, contact information, etc. You don't have to add this, so don't add any sensitive information

8 The default setting on Hotmail is to share your profile information publicly with anyone who has a Windows Live account. To change this, click on the link that currently reads **Everyone (public)** under **Contact info**

9 Untick the box that says **Everyone (public)**. Tick the box that reads **My network**, which mean your information is not accessible to others (only your contacts). Click **Save**

Email

USE HOTMAIL

Once you've set up your webmail account, you'll want to send emails. Find out the email addresses of some family and friends and you're ready to get started.

Send an email

1 Go to home.live.com. Log into your Hotmail account with your email address and password

2 To send an email click **New** at the top of the screen or press **Ctrl + N**

3 Type the email address of the recipient in the **To** box (for example, JohnSmith@hotmail.com) or click on **To:** to reveal any friends' addresses you have added to your **Contacts** (see page 141)

4 Enter a subject line for your email and type your text

5 Click **Send**

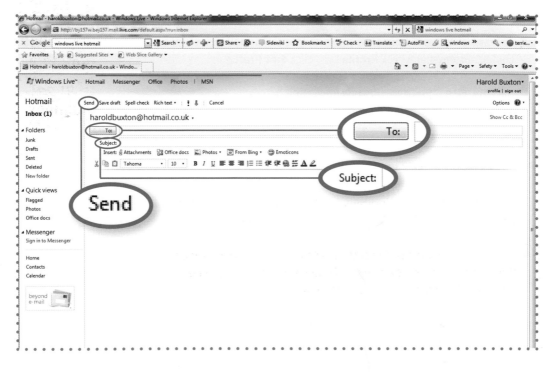

Create a new folder

Your inbox can quickly become full of emails, but creating folders, in which you can store your emails if you want to keep them can soon help to organise things.

1 Click **New folder**

2 Enter a name for your new folder

3 If you want the folder to be visible at all times in the left-hand folder menu, click **Save**. This will make it a 'top-level' folder

4 Or if you want your new folder to sit within another folder, click on the arrow for a drop-down menu of options. From here you can create a new folder within your existing folder

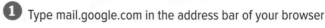Email

CREATE A GMAIL ACCOUNT

1 Type mail.google.com in the address bar of your browser

2 Click **Create an account**

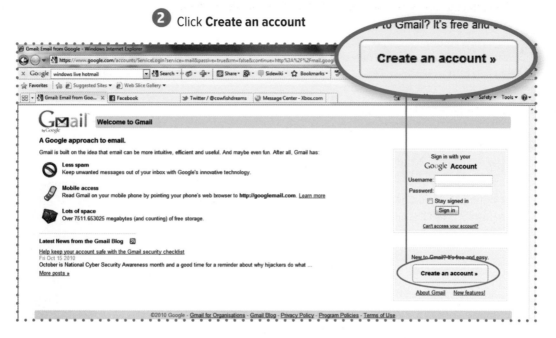

3 This will open a registration page asking you to fill in your details. If your chosen name isn't available, you'll have to enter an alternative. Once you've done this, click **I Accept/Create my Account**

4 Once your account is created, go to the web page mail.google.com to log into your account

Send an email on Gmail

1 Enter your username and password

2 Click **Sign in**

3 Click on **Compose Mail** (top left of the screen) to write an email

4 Enter the email address of the recipient in the 'To' box, and add a subject

5 When you've written your email, click **Send**

Send instant messages to friends on Google Mail

1 If you have friends that also use Gmail you can invite them to chat. Some of your contacts may already appear in the menu on the left-hand side, under 'Chat'

2 To invite someone to chat, enter his or her email address in the box under 'Chat'

3 Press **Enter** and click **Invite to chat**

4 To chat with a friend, make sure they are online (when they are also logged into Google Mail they will have a green dot next to their name) and click on their name to open a window where you can type your messages. Each time you press return, your message will show up on your friend's screen

⏵ Email

EMAIL CLIENTS

An email client is a program used to manage and send emails. Previous versions of Windows came with an email client pre-installed, but with Windows 7, you have the option to download one yourself, as part of the Windows Live Essentials package.

Windows Live Essentials is a collection of free programs, including Windows Live Mail, Photo Gallery and Movie Maker.

GET WINDOWS LIVE ESSENTIALS

1 Click ⊞ and type Windows Live Essentials in the Search box

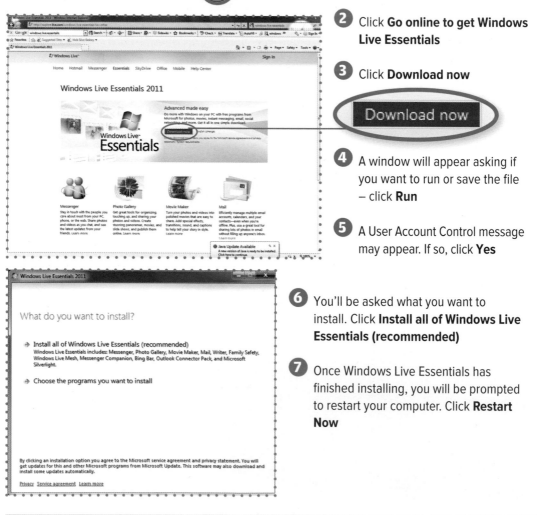

2 Click **Go online to get Windows Live Essentials**

3 Click **Download now**

4 A window will appear asking if you want to run or save the file – click **Run**

5 A User Account Control message may appear. If so, click **Yes**

6 You'll be asked what you want to install. Click **Install all of Windows Live Essentials (recommended)**

7 Once Windows Live Essentials has finished installing, you will be prompted to restart your computer. Click **Restart Now**

SETTING UP WINDOWS LIVE MAIL

1 Click [icon], then click **All programs**

2 Click **Windows Live Mail**

3 If you already have an email address, enter it in the window that appears

4 If you don't have an email address, click **Get a Windows Live email address**

5 You'll now be prompted to create a Windows Live ID. Enter all of your details (see page 128)

6 Now that you have an email address you can enter it in step 4. Click **Next**

7 Click **Finish**

8 Windows Live Mail will now synchronise with your Windows Live ID

9 You may be prompted to confirm your user name and password. Click **OK**

135

Email

Main toolbar
Buttons for the main functions, such as sending and receiving mail, creating new messages and replying to or forwarding mail.

USING WINDOWS LIVE MAIL

When you open Windows Mail it will check to see if you've got any messages and download these to your inbox (if you're connected to the internet). Then it will check every half hour (by default) for any new messages. If you want to check in between, you can do this manually by following these steps:

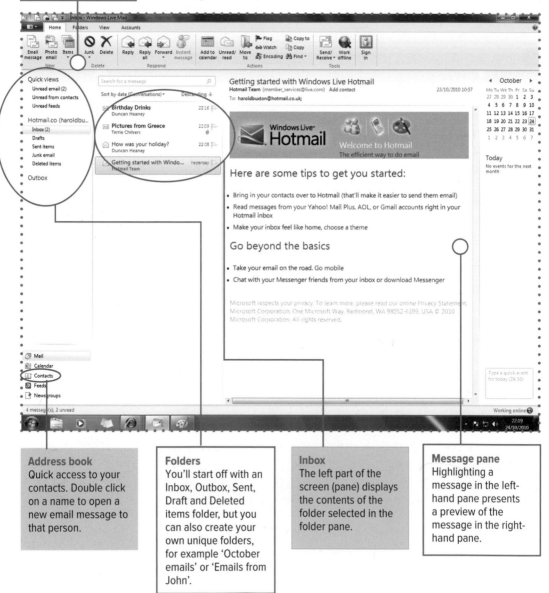

Address book
Quick access to your contacts. Double click on a name to open a new email message to that person.

Folders
You'll start off with an Inbox, Outbox, Sent, Draft and Deleted items folder, but you can also create your own unique folders, for example 'October emails' or 'Emails from John'.

Inbox
The left part of the screen (pane) displays the contents of the folder selected in the folder pane.

Message pane
Highlighting a message in the left-hand pane presents a preview of the message in the right-hand pane.

1 Make sure you're connected to the internet

2 Select **Send/Receive**

3 Click **Send and Receive All**

4 Any new messages will arrive in your inbox

Open and read an email

1 Select **Inbox** from the folders list

2 Click once on the message you want to read and it will appear in the right half of the screen automatically

3 To open the message in a separate, bigger window, double click on the message

TIP
Press **F5** to automatically refresh your inbox.

TIP
Forwarding an email is sending an email you've received on to another recipient (see page 139).

▶ Email

Write and send an email

1 Click **Email message**

Email message

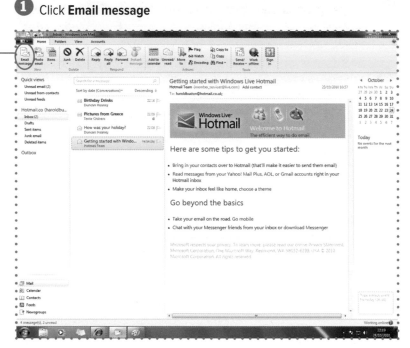

2 A new window will appear

3 In the **To** box, type the email address of the person you're writing to. Or you can use your address book/contacts (see page 141)

4 As well as the **To** field, most email programs have **CC** (carbon copy) and **BCC** (blind carbon copy) fields that allow you to copy your email to others. When you use the CC field, all recipients are aware who has received a copy of the email. The BCC field can be used if you don't want any of the recipients to know who else the email has been copied to

TIP
If you can't see the **CC** and **BCC** fields then click **View** and then **All Headers.**

5 In the **Subject** box, type a title for your message

6 In the box below, type your message

7 When you're finished, click **Send**

Reply to and forward an email

1 To reply to a message, open the message and click **Reply**. This will automatically open a new window (with the recipient's email address already entered) where you can write your email

2 To forward a message, open the message and click **Forward**. This will open a new window where you can write your email. You will need to enter the recipient's email address (see opposite)

Delete an email

1 In your inbox, click once on the message you want to delete

2 On the toolbar click **Edit**, then **Delete**

3 Alternatively, in the inbox, right click on the message and click **Delete**

4 To select multiple messages, hold down the **Ctrl** key while you click each message you want to delete until they're all highlighted. Then follow step 2

Attach a file to an email

1 Once you've written your email click the **Attach File to Message** button

2 Locate the file you want to send (see page 13) and click on it (photographs are likely to be in your Pictures folder)

3 Click **Open**

4 The file will appear in the **Attach** box

5 Click **Send**

TIP
If you want to send an email to more than one person, type a semi-colon between email addresses.

TIP
Change the font size, style or colour in your email by clicking on the buttons on the toolbar above your message.

Open an attachment

1 Open the message that contains an attachment by double clicking on it

2 Double click on the file attachment icon at the top of the new message window

3 The attachment will open in a new window. Then you can save it (see page 37 for more on saving)

4 If the attachment is a picture, it should automatically display in the email. If not, follow the same steps as above.

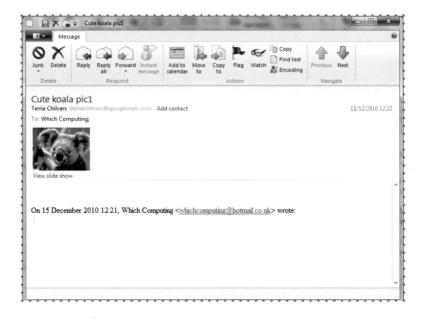

ADD AN ADDRESS TO WINDOWS CONTACTS

Windows Contacts acts as an address book where you can store the details of people you know. Once you've added a contact, you won't need to type out their email address when you use Windows Mail. Here's how to add a contact:

1 Click **Contacts**

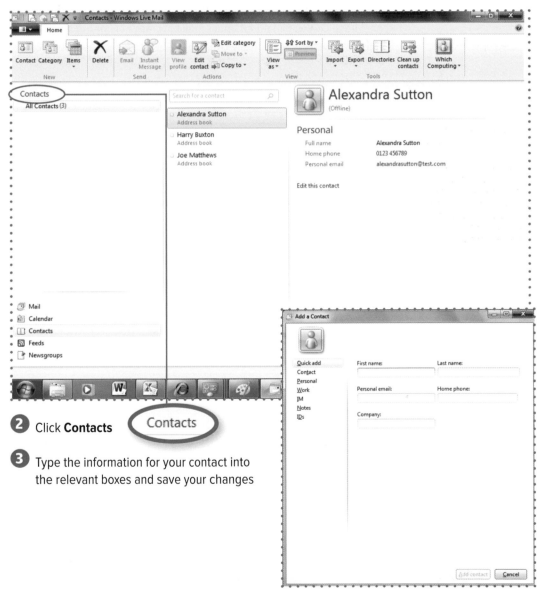

2 Click **Contacts**

3 Type the information for your contact into the relevant boxes and save your changes

DEAL WITH SPAM

Spam is the electronic equivalent of junk mail. It can clog up your inbox with rubbish and make it hard to sift through messages. Spam emails can also contain offensive material and are often the carriers of viruses and phishing scams.

Some internet service providers automatically use spam filters on their email server to try to prevent this; webmail accounts usually also feature spam filters. Or you can adapt your email program to filter out certain types of message automatically by changing your junk email settings.

Filter junk mail in Windows Live Mail (Hotmail)

1 Click **Options** in the top right of your screen

2 Click **More options**

3 Under **Junk Mail**, click **Filters and Reporting**

4 From the list that appears, you can select how your account deals with junk mail

5 Click **Save** when you've made your changes

Filter junk mail in Windows Mail

 Click **Junk** (the red circle with the diagonal red line though it – see opposite highlighted in yellow)

 A window will appear. Here you can choose the level of protection you want

3 Make your choices and click **OK**

TOP TIPS FOR AVOIDING SPAM

▶ Don't reply to spam emails. Replying to spam emails confirms to the sender that your email address is genuine. Clicking on an 'unsubscribe' link in a spam email will have the same effect. Simply delete them without opening

▶ Create a separate email to use for online shopping, using forums and signing up for services – something like a free Windows Live Hotmail account (http://mail.live.com) that you can always scrap and start again

▶ Choose a complicated email address. Picking an obscure email address can help prevent spammers from sending anything to you

▶ The best way to keep the junk at bay is to use a dedicated spam filter. The best spam tools use a white list for 'good' email addresses and a black list for addresses, keywords and phrases that you don't want in your inbox. Most email accounts include a spam filter, but there are also dedicated spam-filtering tools available, including free downloadable spam filters like Mailwasher (www.mailwasher.net) and SpamFighter (www.spamfighter.com)

▶ Report spam to your internet service provider or webmail service provider. This can help your provider to determine and eliminate future spam emails. Often you can do this by clicking **Report this email as junk** when prompted

NEXT STEP

Spam emails can try to lure you into phishing scams. Read more about how to avoid these on page 144.

AVOID PHISHING SCAMS

Phishing refers to cons where unwitting victims are hooked into handing over personal information on email – bank account details, passwords, credit card numbers and the like – by criminals who sell on this data or make use of it themselves to commit fraud.

Phishing scams frequently take the form of a hoax spam email that looks like it came from an official source, such as your bank or building society. The email may ask you to email back personal account details. Often the email asks you to click on a link within the message. The link takes you to a fake website that looks practically indistinguishable from the real thing. Entering any login details, bank account numbers or any personal info into such a web page will hand your sensitive data right into the hands of identity thieves.

The best thing to do is delete any suspicious emails and avoid any suspicious sites. However, there are also dedicated filters that can help you to spot the scams.

PHISHING FILTERS

Most web browsers have built-in tools for spotting fake sites and potentially dangerous phishing web pages. Most of these phishing filters work by comparing the site you're visiting against a list of known hoax pages, and then warning you if it looks like the web address you're visiting might be fraudulent.

Turn on the phishing filter in Internet Explorer

1 Go to **Tools**

2 Click **SmartScreen Filter**

3 Click **Turn on SmartScreen Filter**

4 Scroll down and ensure there's a tick next to **Turn on automatic website checking**

5 Click **OK**

Report a potential hoax website in Internet Explorer

1 While on the suspect page, click **Tools**

2 Click **SmartScreen Filter**

3 Select **Report Unsafe Website**

4 A new window will open showing the address of the site. Tick next to **I think this is a phishing website**

5 Type the characters that you can see in the box at the bottom

6 Click **Submit**

Turn on the phishing filter in Firefox

1 Go to **Tools**

2 Click **Options**

3 Under the **Security** tab, make sure there's a tick next to where it says **Tell me if the site I'm visiting is a suspected forgery**

Report a potential hoax website in Firefox

1 With the page open, go to **Help**

2 Click **Report Web Forgery**

3 This will bring up a web page where you can report the suspected site

4 Add a comment if you want to and click **Submit Report**

email

HOW TO SPOT A PHISHING SCAM

which?
bank*

Logos
These might look like the real deal, but logos are easily copied and are not a guarantee of authenticity.

Dear Valued Customer

We recently have determined that different computers have logged into your Which? Bank account, and multiple password failures were present before the logons.

In this manner for your security, your specified access account has been locked and needs to be reactivated, in order for it to remain active, please Use the link below to proceed and unlock your account.

So we want you to use this oppurtunity to upgrade your account to our new security with the Which? Bank.

https://www.mybank.which/index.asp?

I am convinced that Which? Bank will be a leading UK bank focused on giving you great service and value-for-money products.

Yours sincerely

Chairman, Which? Bank

This message was sent to you as a Which? Bank customer, to inform you regarding important information about your account.

Impersonal
The email might be addressed to 'dear valued customer' or 'valued client'. Genuine emails from your bank will usually address you by name.

Scare tactics
To frighten you into taking action they might tell you that someone has tried to access your bank fraudulently and that you must login now to verify your personal details or your account will be closed.

Spelling/grammar
There might be spelling mistakes, poor syntax (such as overuse of capital letters), or wording may be overcomplicated.

The small print
This might look genuine but it could easily be copied from a genuine email so is not a guarantee of authenticity.

Link
They will send you an emailed link to a fraudulent web page. This may look suspicious or it may be exactly the same address as the genuine login page. Never click on an emailed link.

*This email and the use of a Which? Bank logo are for illustrative purposes only.

EMAIL ETIQUETTE

The top ten dos and don'ts when it comes to sending emails.

▶ Do tone it down. Avoid capital letters. They are harder to read and are the email equivalent of shouting at someone, which may cause offence

▶ Do respect privacy. When sending out a group email, put all the email addresses in the blind carbon copy (BCC) field rather than the To or CC fields. That way, you'll be respecting the privacy of all the people on your recipient list by keeping their email addresses hidden from all the others

▶ Do double check all addresses you enter manually to ensure your message doesn't end up going to the wrong person

▶ Do try to make sure the subject field of your emails contains something meaningful to help your recipient know what the email is about

▶ Do use your email program's spellchecker before you hit send – particularly for more formal communications

▶ Don't open any email attachments unless you're 100 per cent sure they are legitimate. If you recognise the name of the person sending you an email but weren't expecting an attachment, check they meant to send it. Some viruses can hijack people's email accounts without their knowledge

▶ Think before you forward something on to other people. If it's a joke, it might not always be appreciated. And, even if you forward something that looks like helpful advice, you could just be helping to perpetuate junk email messages

▶ Don't overdo it. You can cheer up your emails with fonts, colours and graphics, but don't go overboard. Less is more – and not everyone's email program will be able to display your formatting

▶ Never include any sensitive personal data in your email messages. Email is not a particularly secure method of communication and therefore not suitable for things like bank details, credit card numbers and passwords

▶ Keep an eye on the size (in KB or MB) of the files you send. Big attachments can be a pain for the person you send them to, as they take much longer to download. A large attachment could also clog up the recipient's mailbox

EMAIL PICTURES

Digital cameras can generate extremely large image files that may clog up another person's inbox if you attach them to an email (see page 147) straight after you've transferred them to your computer. The large size of an image might also mean it gets sent straight to the recipient's junk mail folder or be blocked altogether. Or, even if they can view the picture, it may be so large that they have to scroll up, down and across to see the whole image.

Fortunately, Windows 7 features a handy tool that allows you to resize pictures for easy sending. This involves altering their resolution. When emailing a picture, consider what the person receiving it wants to do with it before choosing an image size (see step 4). Anything less than 1MB is fine to send via email.

1 Open **Windows Photo Gallery**

2 Click on the picture you want to email

3 Click **Email** at the top of the window

4 Choose the picture size you want from the drop-down menu The 'smaller' size is fine if the recipient will only be looking at the photos on screen, while 'small' is suitable for printing photos sized 4 x 6 inches. Both 'medium' and 'large' are suitable for printing photos sized 5 x 7 inches

5 Once you've selected the size, you'll see the estimated size of your attachment

6 If it's OK, click **Attach**

NEXT STEP ▶

You don't have to email photos to share them with a friend – you can post them on a photo-sharing website where you can invite friends to view them (see page 160).

NEXT STEP ▶

For more on attaching files to emails, see page 139.

VIDEO CHAT ONLINE

You can make phone calls online to friends and family with a headset/
microphone, or even video chat if you have a webcam. One of the most
popular websites to use is Skype.

Download and install Skype

1 Open your web browser and type www.skype.com into the address
bar. Press **Enter**

2 Click **Join Skype**

3 When the **File Download** dialogue box appears, click **Run**

4 Click **I agree – install** in the window that appears

5 Once the file has downloaded, click **Finish**

⏵ Chat Online

TRY THIS

If a warning appears when you try to download Skype, check at the top of the window. Your web browser may be blocking the download. Click on the warning bar and click **Download file**.

Create an account

1 Once you've finished installing the software, there will be a **Thank You** screen. Click **Start Skype**

2 In the **Create Account** window that opens, enter your name and choose a Skype name and password

3 Check the tick box and click **Next**

4 Fill out your email address on the next screen and enter your Country/Region and your nearest city

5 Finally, check or uncheck the boxes as required and click **Sign In**

Set up

1 When you first sign into Skype, the **Getting Started** wizard will launch. Before you continue, connect your headset or handset if you're using one

2 If you're using a standard microphone headset, you should find it has two plugs attached to it. Insert the pink or red one into your computer's microphone socket (this should also be pink/red or marked with the icon of a microphone)

3 Plug the green one into the headphone output (also green or marked with a stereo sound waves icon)

Make a test call

1 You'll find a Skype Test Call contact listed in your Skype contacts. To make your test call, click the green **Call button** next to this contact

2 You should hear instructions prompting you to record a message after the beep

3 You should then be able to hear the message you recorded. If you can't, onscreen instructions will tell you what to do (you may need a headset if you don't have one already)

Add contacts

 Ask your friends to send you their Skype names. You can then add them to your Skype contacts by clicking **Add a contact** (the little green circle with a plus sign and a contact icon)

Add a contact

If they're on Skype too, calls are free.

Enter all the details you know:

Email

Phone number

Full name

Skype Name

Add

TIP

Phone calls between Skype users are free, regardless of where in the world you're phoning.

 Alternatively you can search for people by adding their email address or name

3 Click **View** to see the search results

Make a Skype call

1 Double click on the Skype icon on your desktop or in the system tray. Select the **Contacts** tab in the main Skype window and scroll down your contacts list until you find the person you want to call

2 Click the green **Call** icon that appears in the right-hand pane. To video call, click the green **Video Call** icon

3 If they aren't listed, type their Skype name (you'll need to get this from the person you want to contact) into the box at the bottom of the Skype window and click the **Search Contact** icon

4 When you receive a call, a window will pop up asking whether you want to accept or reject it. You must be logged in to Skype to receive a call

NEXT STEP ►

You can call a landline or mobile using your Skype account, but you'll need to buy Skype credits. Go to **Account** and click **Buy Skype Credit**. A wizard will launch that will take you through the process. Then, to make a call, click on the **Call Phones** tab in the main Skype window.

⏵ Chat Online

SET UP A WEBCAM

Webcams send moving images of you to another webcam-equipped computer via the internet. It's an effective way to stay in touch with friends and loved ones. Both you and the person you're talking to will need a webcam and a broadband connection. If you have a new PC/laptop it may have an integrated webcam in the screen; if not, you'll need to invest in a separate webcam. Here's how to attach a webcam to your monitor.

1 Run the setup CD included with the webcam (if there is one). This will install the drivers that the webcam needs to work with your computer

2 Cameras clip or rest on top of your PC. Refer to your webcam manual for specific instructions

3 Place your webcam at around eye level and an arm's length from your face to ensure that people aren't squinting to see you or staring up your nose

4 When prompted, plug the webcam into your USB port. Windows 7 should recognise it and the software will set up the webcam's built in microphone and the camera

5 Most webcam software provides shortcuts to the popular instant messaging services Windows Live! Messenger and Skype, and often links to Yahoo! Messenger and AOL's AIM too

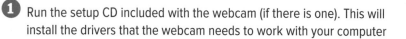

PHOTOS, VIDEOS & MUSIC

By reading this chapter you will get to grips with:

 Organising your digital photos

 Editing video clips

 Downloading music

▶ Photos

IMPORT PICTURES FROM A DIGITAL CAMERA TO A COMPUTER

Digital cameras make it easier to take pictures and to then store and circulate them electronically via your PC. Follow these instructions to transfer your pictures from a digital camera to your computer.

1 Connect the camera to your PC using a USB cable or, if your PC has a compatible card slot, you can pop the card from your camera straight into your PC. Your camera's instruction booklet will help you

2 Windows will present you with a window titled **Autorun**. Click **Import pictures using Windows**

3 Windows will save the photos from the memory card into your **Pictures** folder

4 You'll be given the option to tag your pictures as you import them. Tags are keywords that you can use to identify and locate photos (for example, you can search for all the photos that you've tagged with 'beach' or a specific person's name). The tags you enter will apply to all the imported photos, so keep them fairly general. More specific tags can be added later on. Click **Import** when you're done

5 Photo Gallery will open automatically to show the pictures

TRANSFER PICTURES USING A SCANNER

Some printers also allow you to scan pictures and documents. Once you've scanned something, you then have an electronic copy that you can send via email or store on your computer. Windows Live Photo Gallery allows you to store and organise your photos – find out how to download it on page 134.

1 Connect the scanner to your PC as explained in the scanner's manual. Then place the photo on the scanner, ensuring the scanner is switched on

2 Click **File**

3 Click **Import from a camera or scanner** from the **Windows Live Photo Gallery** toolbar

4 Double click the scanner icon and click **Import**

5 Customise any settings (such as size and colour) and click **Scan**

TRANSFER PICTURES FROM ANOTHER FOLDER TO THE PHOTO GALLERY

You may have pictures in another folder that you want to move to Windows Photo Gallery. Follow these steps to transfer them:

1 In the photo gallery, click **File**

2 Click **Include a folder** in the gallery

3 Find the folder you want to add (see page 156 for more on locating pictures)

4 Click **OK** and then **OK** again

photos

⊳ Photos

SAVE AND ORGANISE PHOTOS

Once you have your photos on your computer, you'll need to sort and manage them. You can use Windows Live Photo Gallery to organise your photos – this is part of the Windows Live Essentials package, which you can download for free (see page 134).

View your photos

1 Click

2 Click **All Programs**

3 Click **Windows Live Photo Gallery**

4 Double click on a picture to see a bigger version. From here you can browse through your pictures by clicking the left and right arrows, or you can view a slideshow (your photos automatically shown onscreen in succession without you having to click each time, allowing you to view them as if you were flicking through a photo album)

TIP

Photo Gallery allows you to email photos from within the program, and can also make them smaller (see page 148).

TIP

Tagging photos makes it easier to search the Windows Live Photo Gallery (see page 154).

⑤ To tag a picture, click **Add descriptive tags**. If you want to add more than one tag, separate each word with a forward slash (/)

⑥ If you can't see this option, click **Info** on the top toolbar

Change how your photos are listed

Photo Gallery organises all your photos by date. You can, however, opt to view your images by other criteria, using the filters on the left-hand side of the window.

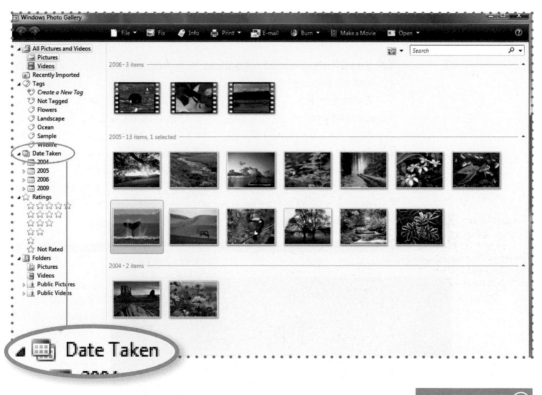

❶ Click on **Date Taken** and select a year to see all the photos from that year

❷ If you have tagged and rated your pictures you can also click on the relevant filter on the left to view photos by keyword or rating

NEXT STEP ⊙

You can use Windows Live Photo Gallery to edit your photos, as well as print, email or burn CDs of all your favourites (see page 158).

photos

▶ Photos

EDIT YOUR PHOTOS

Once you've added your photos to the Windows Live Photo Gallery, you can use a number of editing tools to improve your pictures. In each case, follow the Preparing to edit steps below, and then choose what you want to do to your picture. For example, you can remove red eye or crop part of a picture.

Preparing to edit

1 Double click on the image you want to edit and click **Fix** on the main toolbar

2 You will see a number of options: Auto Adjust, Exposure, Colour, Crop and Fix Red Eye

Remove red eye

1 To remove part of a picture, click **Crop picture**

2 To remove red-eye click on **Fix Red Eye**, then use the mouse pointer to drag a small rectangle around the eye you want to fix. Repeat as necessary. Remember to save a copy of your edited photo

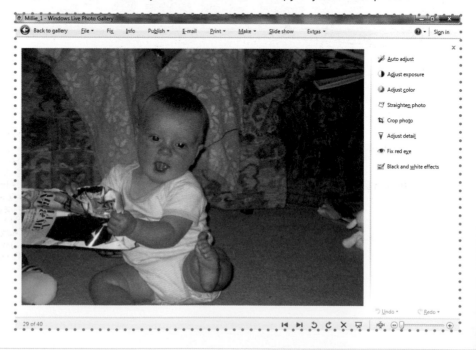

Crop your photo

1 To remove part of a picture, click **Crop photo**

2 A frame will appear on the picture. What's inside the frame represents the part of your picture you will retain when you crop it. Drag the edges of the frame to adjust it

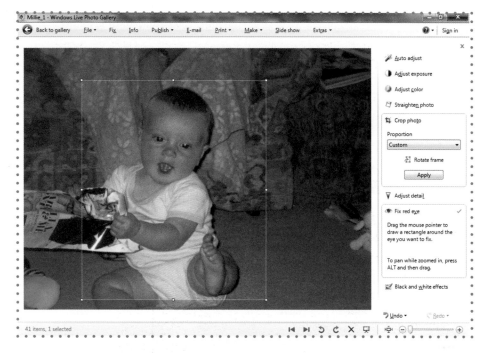

3 Click **Apply**

4 You'll see the new cropped version of your picture

5 Click **Undo** if you're not happy with the result. Or save a copy of your new picture if you are

TRY THIS

While Photo Gallery allows you to carry out simple fixes, for more advanced features you may want to invest in a separate image-editing software package. For more information, see *Digital Photography Made Easy*, also published by Which? Books.

USE A PHOTO-SHARING SITE

Rather than emailing specific pictures, you can post your photographs online, from where friends and family (with details of the site) can see them. Flickr is a photo-sharing website that allows you to do that.

Create an account

1 You need a Yahoo! Account to use Flickr. To create one, go to the Flickr website www.flickr.com and click **Create your account**

2 This takes you to the Yahoo! sign-up page. Click **Sign Up** (on the bottom right-hand side of the page)

3 Enter your personal details then click **Create My Account**

4 Back on www.flickr.com, log in to Flickr using your Yahoo! account details

5 Select a screen name and click on **Create a new account**

Upload photographs

1 On the welcome screen click **Upload** in the top right of the screen

2 Select **Choose photos and videos**. This will open a window that will enable you to browse your computer for your photos

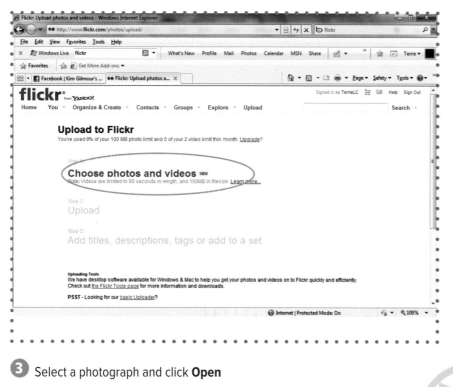

3 Select a photograph and click **Open**

4 Your photo will now be listed on the Flickr web page

5 Select whether you want this picture to be private, whether you want your friends and family to be able to view it, or whether to make it public and allow all Flickr users to see it

6 Click **Upload Photos and Videos**

7 Click **Add a description** if you want to edit the title, add a description or add tags

8 Once you've done this, click **Save**

TIP

When you're logged in, to see your Flickr page click **Your Photostream** on the main page.

▶ Photos

TRY THIS

To put your pictures into a set (a folder where you can group certain photos, such as from one specific occasion), click **Organize**. Drag the photos you want to combine into a set into the grey space. When ready, click **Add to Set**. Fill in a title and description and click **Save**.

Allow others to see your photos

You can also share your photos on Flickr with family and friends who don't have a Flickr account.

1 When you're logged in on the Flickr website, click **Your Photostream**

2 Click **Share this** on the right-hand side

3 Enter the email address of the person you want to view your photos

4 If some of your photos aren't set to public (see Step 5 on page 161), you will have the option to give a guest pass. Tick **Friends and Family** if you want to share all the photos in your photo stream

5 Click **Send**

6 Alternatively, click **Grab the link** and you can then copy the link to pass on to family and friends

COPY YOUR PICTURES TO A DISC

Once you've organised and edited your photos on your computer, you may want to save them onto a CD or DVD to share with friends or so that you have a backup copy.

1 Insert a blank or re-writeable CD or DVD into your computer

2 Open **Windows Photo Gallery**. Choose the photos you want to save by holding down the **Ctrl** button on your keyboard and single-clicking on each one in the main **Gallery** window

3 Click **Burn a DVD**

4 Click **Next**

5 Click **Burn**

UPLOAD VIDEO FOOTAGE ON TO YOUR PC

A camcorder is great for capturing precious memories, whether it's a party for a golden wedding anniversary or a special holiday. Sometimes, however, your footage may be too long, or include sections you'd rather cut.

To edit your video, you'll first need to transfer your footage onto your computer. In some cases you may be required to use the software provided with your camcorder to do this, but the instructions will be similar to those below.

1 Connect your camcorder to your computer with a USB or firewire cable

2 Turn on your camcorder and set it to playback mode (this is often labelled VTR or VCR but will depend on the type of camcorder)

3 A box titled **Autoplay** will appear. Click **Import Video**

4 Choose where you want to save your video file from the **Import** to list

5 In the **Format** list, choose which video file format you want your video to be saved as. If you will want to create one file from your video, select **Windows Media File (single file)**

6 Click **Next**

7 Click **Import the entire videotape to my computer**

8 Click **Next**. If you want to stop importing video before the end of the tape, click **Stop** and then **Yes**

9 Click **Finish**. Your video has now been converted into a video file that you can edit

videos

TIP
As well as recording video on a camcorder, most digital cameras allow you to record video clips.

Jargon buster

Firewire
A type of connection that can quickly transfer large amounts of data, such as video footage, between your computer and other devices.

TRY THIS
Video consumes more storage space than any other type of media file. Therefore, while not essential, it's preferable to store it on a separate hard drive (see pages 186–7) if you plan on editing a lot of material.

REMEMBER
It's important to choose the right settings for a project as it can't be altered later. This can usually be done from the Setup menu. UK based camcorders are 'PAL' format; you may also need to check the camcorder documentation to be sure of the format (such as MiniDV/HDV). If the footage was shot in a widescreen mode, choose the relevant '16:9' preset to ensure the video maintains its correct proportions.

▶ Videos

VIDEO-EDITING SOFTWARE

Once you've saved your video clips onto your computer, you can edit them using video-editing software and create a new and improved piece of video. Most packages will also help you create a DVD.

When editing, you can delete sections of video, move parts around, add special effects and transitions between clips, and more. You can also add a soundtrack or narrative to your video, and even create a DVD, complete with a menu, for easy navigation on your TV.

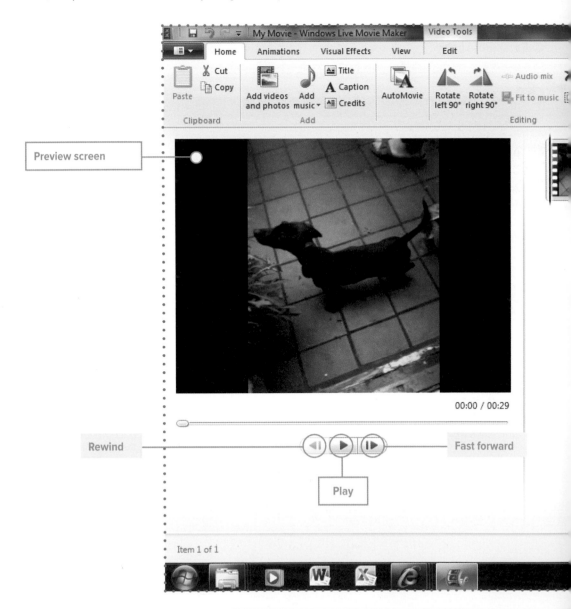

Basic video-editing software is often supplied with your camera or camcorder. Alternatively, you can download Windows Live Essentials (see page 134), which includes video-editing software, Windows Live Movie Maker. This offers most of the more common functions but, if you want something with more features, you can buy a more advanced software package.

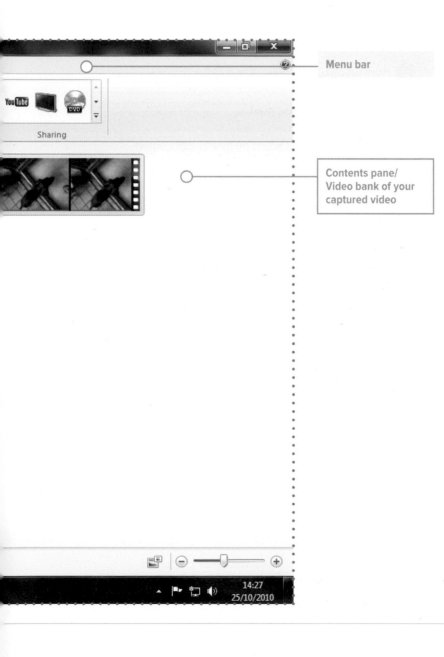

Menu bar

Contents pane/
Video bank of your
captured video

Sharing

14:27
25/10/2010

Videos

EDIT A VIDEO

Get started

Before you can start editing your video, you need to add the clips you want to use to the timeline.

1 Click

2 Click **All programs**

3 Click **Windows Live Movie Maker**

4 Click **Add videos and photos**

5 Select the video clip you want to add. Click **Open**

6 Your clip will appear in the right-hand pane and you can click play on the preview screen to watch it

7 Repeat steps 4 and 5 to add more video clips

8 This is the best time to put your clips in the order that you want them to be watched. Do this by dragging and dropping clips in the right-hand pane. To drag and drop, keep the mouse button pressed down as you drag it to the timeline. Let go at the location you want to drop it

TIP
If you want to undo something you've done, press **Ctrl + Z**.

Trim a clip

If some of your scenes are too long, they can be trimmed before being edited into a whole.

1 Click **Edit** on the toolbar. Click **Trim tool**

2 On the video in the right-hand side, drag the line to where you want to start the clip you want to save

3 Click **Set start point**

4 Drag the line to where you want your clip to end

5 Click **Set end point**

Split a clip

If you want to add an effect between scenes – for example, you might want to fade out and then fade in (see page 168) – you'll first need to split your clip.

1 Click **Edit** on the toolbar

2 On the video in the right-hand side, drag the line to the point where you want to split your clip

3 Click **Split**

TIP

Right click on a clip in the right-hand pane to reveal a menu of actions, including Copy, Paste and Remove.

4 The two parts will now appear separately

BE CAREFUL

With every major change that you make, save a copy of your project so you don't lose it (see page 170).

Videos

Add transitions

A video can look a little clunky if the scenes are just sandwiched together. You can avoid this by adding transitions, such as a fade-in or fade-out effect. These are placed between the clips on the timeline.

1 On the timeline, click on the clip that you want to appear after the transition

2 Click **Animations**

3 Select a transition and how long you want it to last (next to **Duration**)

TIP

To preview your video at any time, click on the **Play** button.

4 Click **Play** on the preview monitor to see a preview of what the transition will look like

5 You can also add a 'fade in' and 'fade out' effect by clicking on **Edit** and then selecting an option from the drop-down menus

Add music

You may want to add music to your video. First, you'll need to add the music to your computer (see page 173), then you can use this in your newly created video.

1 Click **Add music**

2 Then select either **Add music** or **Add music at the current point**

3 Find the file that you want to add and click on it. Any audio is likely to be stored in your Music folder

4 Click **Open**

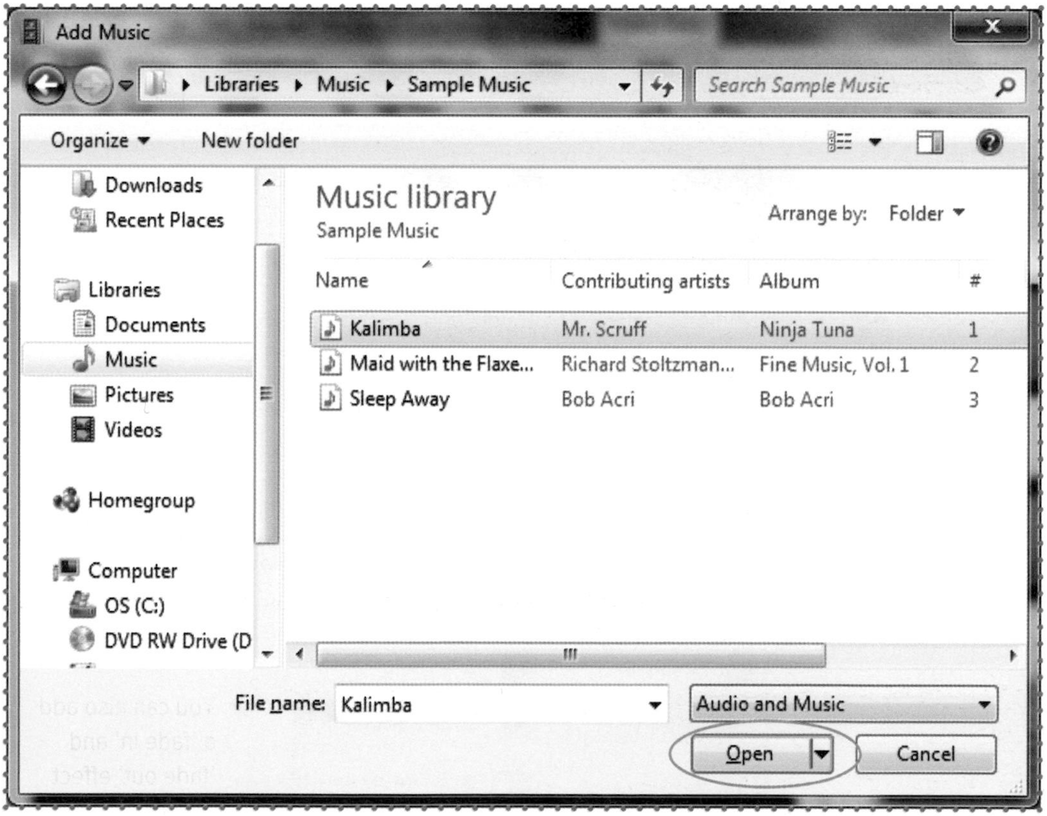

TRY THIS

At any point you can tweak the properties of an element of your project (clip, audio track, sound effects, transitions) by hovering the mouse cursor over it and right-clicking.

5 The music file will appear alongside your clip in the right-hand pane

▶ Videos

Save an edited video

You should save your edited video (known as a project) regularly, so that you don't lose any of your changes should something go wrong.

 Click the down arrow to the left of the Home tab on the toolbar

2 Click **Save Project As** if you haven't already given your project a name, name it and then **Save**

3 If you've already given your video a name, simply click **Save Project**

Publish and share a video

Saving your project just saves the settings and instructions on how you would like your finished video to look. To create a file of your completed video that you can watch and share with others you will need to publish your clip.

1 Click the down arrow to the left of the Home tab on the toolbar

2 Click **Save Movie**

3 Select which format you would like to save your video in

4 Click the folder where you want to save your video

5 Type a name for your video in the box that appears

6 Click **Save** and wait while your video is published. Depending on the length of your video this could take a little while

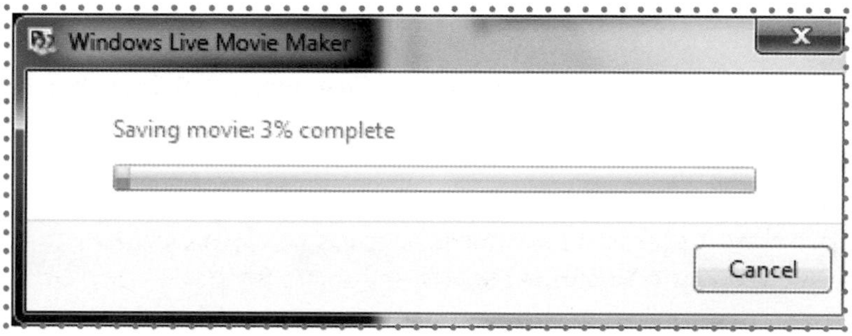

Windows Live Movie Maker   **X**

Saving movie: 3% complete

[   ]

                                                    Cancel

BE CAREFUL
Once you've published your video you can't edit it. You can only edit the saved project so make sure you're happy with it first.

7 Once your video has been published, click **Close** or click **Play** to watch your video

▶ Videos

CREATE A DVD OF YOUR VIDEO

To burn a video to DVD, your computer needs to have a rewriteable disc drive – look for the RW logo on your disc drive. You can create a DVD using Windows Live Movie Maker.

1 Click the DVD icon in the toolbar (in the 'Sharing' section)

TRY THIS

You can also use Windows DVD Maker to create DVDs. This is included with Windows 7 – click **Start**, then **All Programs** and finally **Windows DVD Maker** to get started.

2 Click **Next**

3 Click on **Menu text** to add a title and **Customize menu** to choose what plays in the background on your DVD's menu screen

4 You can also choose a menu style in the right-hand section

5 Click **Preview** if you want to see what your video looks like before you create your DVD

6 Click **Burn** and wait while your DVD is created

PLAY MUSIC

You can play a CD through your computer, in the same way as you would on your stereo. To play, put a CD in the CD drive and wait while the default music player on your computer starts up. This is likely to be Windows Media Player.

Press play or double click on a particular track to listen to your CD.

TRY THIS

When you put a CD into your computer, a window may appear asking how you'd like to play the CD. Click Play using **Windows Media Player.**

music

Library
The music you have stored on your computer will appear here.

Volume
Alter the volume by dragging the dot.

Burn
Copy music on to a CD. To do this you'll need a rewriteable disc drive.

Sync
Transfer music from an MP3 player to Windows Media Player.

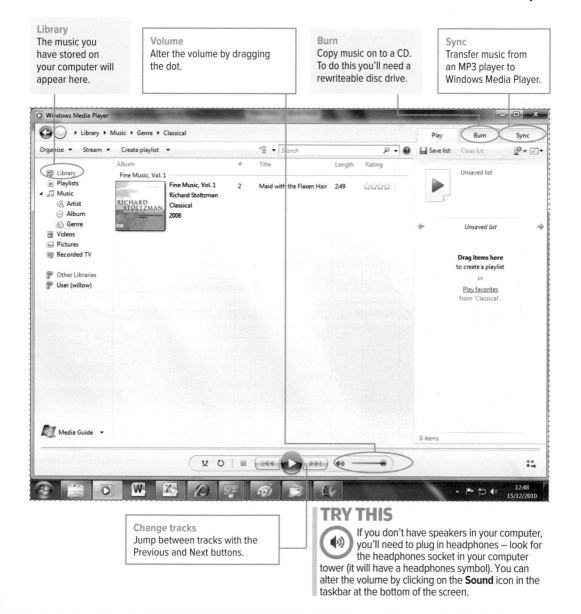

Change tracks
Jump between tracks with the Previous and Next buttons.

TRY THIS

If you don't have speakers in your computer, you'll need to plug in headphones – look for the headphones socket in your computer tower (it will have a headphones symbol). You can alter the volume by clicking on the **Sound** icon in the taskbar at the bottom of the screen.

 # Music

BE CAREFUL

For tips on shopping safely online see page 107.

DOWNLOAD MUSIC

As well as playing CDs on your computer, you can also download music from the internet. You can buy individual music tracks or even whole albums from sites such as iTunes, HMV and Tesco. For example, with HMV:

1 Go to www.hmvdigital.com

2 Click on the song or album you want to buy

3 Click **Add to basket**

4 When you've finished shopping, click **Checkout**

5 If you haven't already got an HMV account, you'll be prompted to sign up for one now

6 Enter your payment details

Transfer your downloaded music to an MP3 player

To transfer your purchased music to your MP3 player you first need to download the HMV download tool.

1 Click **Get the new hmvdigital download manager**

2 Click **Install now**

3 Click **Yes** if you're asked to install Adobe AIR

4 Click **Install** and then **Continue**

5 Click on **I agree** if you're happy with the terms and conditions

6 Click **Yes**

7 Click **English** and then the arrow icon

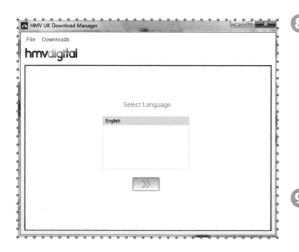

TRY THIS

You can also download 'podcasts' – radio programmes and TV clips – to listen to on your MP3 player or computer. Many of these are free. Take a look at www.apple.com/ podcasting to get started.

8 If you use iTunes tick the first box, or if you want to add your music to your computer's music folder, tick **I'll manage my downloads**

9 Click **OK**. Your music will now appear on iTunes or in your music folder

NEXT STEP

Find out how to transfer music from your computer onto your MP3 player on page 179.

Music

HOW TO SET UP AN ITUNES ACCOUNT

If you own an Apple iPod or listen to music on your PC or Mac, then the chances are you've downloaded and installed the latest version of iTunes. On the left-hand column of the iTunes player you will see a button that says iTunes Store. This is Apple's online digital media store that sells songs, albums, TV shows, movies and movie rentals, and audiobooks. It offers free podcasts and other educational content.

Download from the iTunes store

To download an item from the iTunes Store, you need an iTunes Store account.

TIP
By default your music will be saved to the Music folder.

1 Open **iTunes**

2 Click **Store** and then **Create Account**

3 Choose either **Create New Account** or enter your existing Apple or .Mac ID or AOL screen name. If you have an Apple ID or AOL screen name, you'll just need to enter your billing information and you'll be able to proceed

4 If you're creating a new account, you'll be asked to agree to the iTunes Store's terms and conditions. Read these, check the box (but see also page 15), then click **Continue**

5 Complete the form to create your free Apple ID (the login you will use with the iTunes Store). Enter the **email address** you want to use for this account, create a password and secret question, and decide if you want to sign up for any of Apple's email newsletters. Once done, click **Continue**

6 On the next screen, decide how you want to pay for purchases at the iTunes Store. This can be a credit card, debit card or PayPal account. Enter the card or account details and the billing address for your card. Click **Continue**. You can now start shopping

CONVERT CDS TO MP3

Extracting the digital audio data from a CD and storing it on your PC is a process known as 'ripping'. You can build up a music library on your computer and then transfer songs to an iPod or similar MP3 portable player, stream your tunes around your home or just listen to them at your desktop.

Rip a CD using iTunes

1 Open **iTunes**

2 Insert a CD into the disc drive

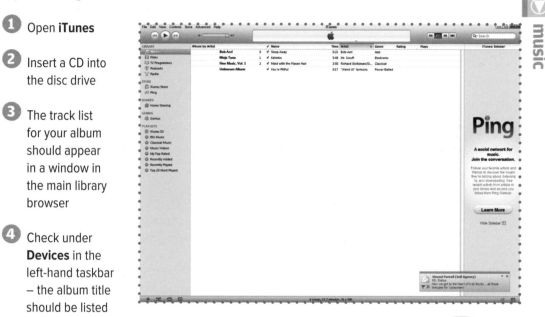

3 The track list for your album should appear in a window in the main library browser

4 Check under **Devices** in the left-hand taskbar – the album title should be listed here next to a small icon representing a compact disc

5 Click **Import CD**

TIP
For advice on installing software like iTunes, see opposite.

Change the format of the file

By default, iTunes converts your CDs to AAC format (see page 182). This is usually fine, but not all programs and devices are compatible with AAC, so you may want to switch to using the more commonly used MP3 format.

1 Go to **Edit**

2 Click **Preferences**

3 On the General tab, click on **Import settings**

4 Under **Import Using** select **MP3 Encoder**

5 Click **OK**

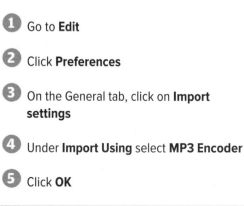

▶ Music

USE AN MP3 PLAYER

MP3 players play music and films that you store digitally. These can either be copies of CDs you already own and have converted to digital files using your computer (see page 173), or music that you've downloaded to your computer from the internet (see page 174).

If you listen to your music on an Apple iPod, you probably use iTunes to manage your music. iTunes is much like Windows Media Player, but with more features, including the ability to download music.

Select your music

1 Open **iTunes** on your computer

2 Connect your music player to your computer. To do this, you'll need to use the lead that came with your player. Connect one end to the correctly shaped socket on your player and connect the other end to your computer's USB socket

3 Wait a few moments. The name of your music player will appear in the list on the left-hand side of the screen under the heading 'devices'

4 The first time you connect your music player to your computer, you'll see a message asking if you want to sync songs automatically. If you say yes, whenever you connect your music player to your computer, any new music that's stored in your iTunes library will automatically be added to your player and any music that you've removed from iTunes will be removed from your player. This is the easiest option

5 It's not always possible to sync everything automatically, though. For example, you might have so many songs in your iTunes library that they won't all fit on your player. If this is the case, you can select individual playlists (see page 180) to add instead

6 With your music player selected in the left-hand panel, click on the **Music** tab

7 Tick the boxes next to the playlists you want to add, tick if you have any music videos you want to add to your playlist too

8 When you're ready, click **Sync**

Transfer music to an MP3 player

1 To add songs to your music player, select **Music** from the list on the left-hand side of the iTunes screen. This brings up the list of all the songs in your iTunes library

2 Select a track by clicking on it and holding down the left-hand mouse button, then dragging it over to where your music player is listed (under Devices). Let go of the mouse button and that track will have been copied onto your music player. You can do the same thing with playlists – click on a playlist, drag it over to where your music player is listed and drop it in

3 If you're managing your music manually as opposed to synching automatically, you'll need to eject your iPod from iTunes before disconnecting. Click on the little upwards facing arrow beside your iPod's name on the iTunes screen and wait for your iPod to say that it's OK to disconnect

▶ Music

CREATE A PLAYLIST

A playlist allows you to group together songs like a compilation.

Using Windows Media Player

1 Click **Playlists**

2 Type in a name for your playlist

3 Add songs by dragging and dropping (see page 12) tracks onto the area below your playlist title (if you can't see your music, click on **Library**)

Using iTunes

You can create a playlist manually using iTunes or you can let iTunes create one for you based on specific criteria.

1 Click **File**

2 Click **New Smart Playlist**

3 A small dialogue box will open and allow you automatically to add songs that match a set of special 'rules'

♫ Smart Playlist		X

☑ Match the following rule:

| Artist ▼ | contains ▼ | [ ] | - | + | ... |

☐ Limit to 25 | items ▼ | selected by | random ▼

☐ Match only ticked items

☑ Live updating

| ? | | OK | Cancel |

4 Choose a rule by selecting criteria from the drop-down menus. For example, select **Genre** from the first list, then **Contains** from the second, then type Classical into the box and click the **plus** ('+') button on the right to create a classical playlist

5 You can add more rules and further refine your playlist by putting a tick next to **Limit to** and setting the size or duration options

6 Click **OK** and type in a name for your playlist

▷ Music

Choosing the right audio format

There are dozens of different digital audio formats knocking around
– such as MP3, WMA, AAC, WAV and Ogg Vorbis – and not all are
compatible with the same media player software or portable music
players. Most downloaded audio, however, is available as either
MP3, AAC and WMA files.

Microsoft and Apple use different audio file types. WMA stands for
Windows Media Audio and is Microsoft's format of choice, while AAC
stands for Advanced Audio Coding and is predominantly used by Apple.
On a PC, you can always download a free software player that supports a
particular format but, before you download any music or podcasts, check
that your player is compatible with that specific format.

Digital rights management

One of the most contentious issues for downloaders is digital rights
management (DRM). This is an anti-piracy technique that allows
companies to retain some control over what you can and can't do with the
file you've downloaded, such as how many times you can copy it either to
a CD or to another machine.

However, it's becoming increasingly easy to find tracks that don't have
DRM restrictions. Many music websites now offer MP3 downloads without
DRM and these tracks can be played on all MP3 players, including iPods.
All the 'big four' record companies (EMI, Universal, Warner and Sony BMG)
have now abandoned DRM.

MAINTAINING YOUR PC

By reading this chapter you will get to grips with:

 Backing up important files

 Cleaning up your desktop

 Uninstalling programs

Backing up Data

BACK UP DATA

It is important to make copies of your important photographs and documents so that you don't lose them should something happen to your computer, like a hard disk failure or virus. You can back up data by saving it to an external hard drive, memory stick or using an online backup service, which saves your data for you online.

SAVE FILES ON A MEMORY STICK

Jargon buster

Memory stick
A small device that plugs into your computer and can be used to save files onto. Also known as a USB key or flash drive.

1 Plug your memory stick into the USB port of your computer

2 Your computer should recognise that you've plugged in an external device. An icon and popup message will appear in the taskbar at the bottom of your screen

3 Open the file you want to save to your memory stick. Click **File**, then **Save As**

4 In the left-hand pane, scroll down to find your USB stick (under 'Computer', and usually called Removable Disk). Click on it

5 Click **Save**

6 To remove the memory stick, click on its icon in the taskbar

7 You may need to click on the up arrow to reveal the icon if it's hidden

ACCESS FILES ON A MEMORY STICK

1 Plug in the memory stick

2 A small window will appear, click **Open folder to view files**

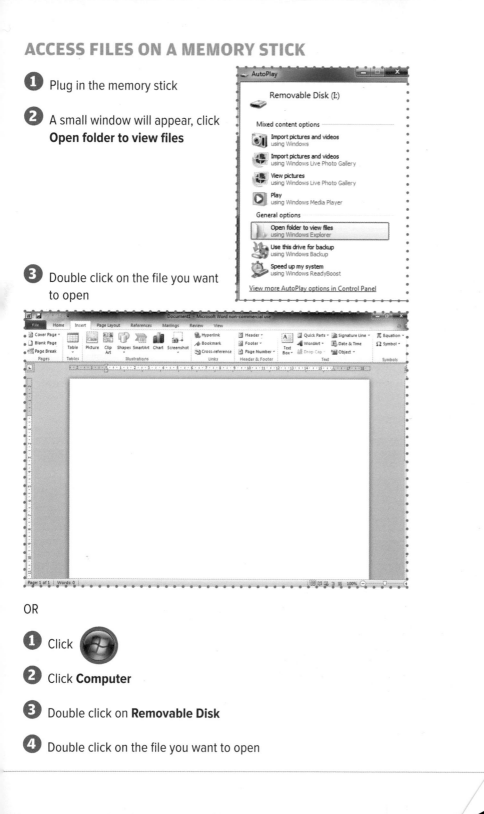

3 Double click on the file you want to open

OR

1 Click

2 Click **Computer**

3 Double click on **Removable Disk**

4 Double click on the file you want to open

▶ Backing up Data

BACK UP FILES

You can use the Windows 7 Backup and Restore tool to back up your important files and set up automatic backups.

1 Click [icon], then **Control Panel**

2 Click **System and Security**

3 Click **Backup and Restore**

4 Click **Set up backup**

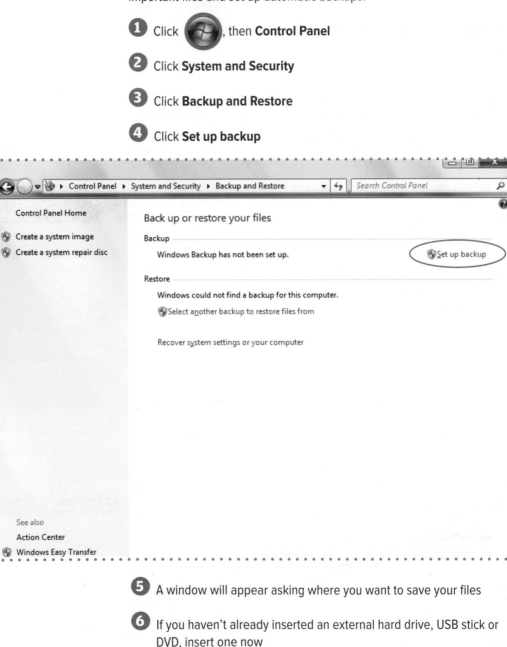

5 A window will appear asking where you want to save your files

6 If you haven't already inserted an external hard drive, USB stick or DVD, insert one now

Once your backup device is inserted

1 Click **Refresh**

2 Click on the backup destination you want to use

3 Click **Next**

4 Now choose which files you want to back up. Either tick **Let Windows choose (recommended)** or **Let me choose** if you want to pick which files and folders to back up. The second option will also allow you to create a system image of your computer (see page 188)

5 Click **Next**

6 You can change when and how frequently the backup takes place by clicking **Change schedule**

7 Click **Save settings and run backup**

8 Should you need to restore files (for example, if you lose a file, it becomes corrupt or is changed accidentally), click **Restore files** when you first open the Backup and Restore window

---

Set up backup

Review your backup settings

Backup Location: Removable Disk (I:)

Backup Summary:

Items	Included in backup
All users	Default Windows folders and lo...

Change schedule

Schedule: Every Sunday at 19:00   Change schedule

Save settings and run backup   Cancel

▶ Backing up Data

FULL-SYSTEM BACKUP

As well as backing up your files, you can back up your entire computer (including the operating system and all programs). This is useful if your computer is affected by a virus and you need to restore everything.

1 Click ![], then **Control Panel**

2 Click **System and Security**

3 Click **Backup and Restore**

4 Click **Create a system image**

5 Saving a system image requires a large storage device, so you will need to connect either an external hard drive or use a number of DVDs

6 Select where you want to save your backup

7 Click **Next**

8 Click **Start backup**

BACKUP TIPS

▶ An external hard drive can be used for backing up data. It connects directly to your PC via a USB cable

▶ You need to make frequent backup copies of any personal files – photos, videos, music, emails, documents, spreadsheets and the like – but you should also consider making a 'full' backup of your PC's system files and installed applications every so often too

▶ When you set your backup schedule, you'll first have to choose exactly what you want to safeguard. You can then schedule your backup frequency. This will depend on the type of data you're protecting – if it's key work documents that change every day, then it's probably worth backing up daily, but if it's a collection of digital photos that only get added to every few weeks, then a weekly backup is sufficient

▶ You can choose between an incremental and full system backup. An incremental backup checks to see which files and folders have been altered since the last time you backed up, and updates your backup copies as necessary. A full system backup makes a 'clone' or disc image of your entire hard drive and enables you to restore your whole system from scratch. The downside of full system backups is that the resulting backup file can be enormous

▶ There are several services that offer online backup, including Carbonite (www.carbonite.com, costing approximately £40 per year)

▶ Blank DVDs are a good way of backing up medium-sized amounts of data (around 4GB per disc). But, as they're prone to getting scratched, they're not as reliable as memory sticks, which can hold more data

DELETE A FILE

Over time, your computer becomes full of old information, such as Word documents and spreadsheets. If you no longer use these, it is worth deleting them to increase the available space for new files you want to create.

1 Click , then **Computer**

2 Navigate to the folder where your file is stored. For example, click on **Documents** in the left-hand pane if you want to delete a Word document

3 Right click on the file and click **Delete**

4 A separate dialogue box will pop up and ask you if you're sure you want to delete the file. Click **Yes**. Your file will now disappear from the folder

USE THE RECYCLE BIN

When you delete a file, it's not deleted forever, but held in the Recycle Bin. You are still able to retrieve files from here, but files in the Recycle Bin are taking up valuable space on your hard drive, so you should clear it out occasionally. To delete a file from the Recycle Bin:

1 Right click on the **Recycle Bin** icon on your desktop

BE CAREFUL

If you accidentally delete a file, you can retrieve it from the Recycle Bin. Double click on the **Recycle Bin** icon. You'll see a list of your deleted files. Right click on the file you want to recover and click **Restore**. The file will reappear in its original location.

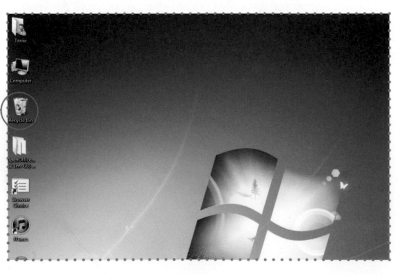

2 Click **Empty Recycle Bin**

3 A window will appear asking if you're sure you want to continue. Click **Yes**

Delete Multiple Items

⚠ Are you sure you want to permanently delete all of these items?

Yes   No

BE CAREFUL

Before emptying the Recycle Bin, make sure there's nothing in there that you want.

▶ Spring-clean your PC

FREE UP SPACE ON YOUR HARD DRIVE

When you're using your computer frequently it can quickly become clogged up with information that can slow it down. You can free up space on your computer's hard drive by using a program called Disk Cleanup, which will remove any temporary files and unnecessary system files, as well as empty your Recycle Bin.

1 Click [image], then **All Programs**

2 Click **Accessories**

3 Click **System Tools**

4 Click **Disk Cleanup**

5 The Disk Cleanup tool will calculate how much space you will be able to free up on your C: drive. This may take a couple of minutes

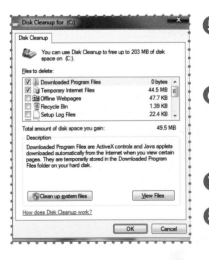

6 Tick **Downloaded Program Files** and **Temporary Internet Files**. If you're not sure what something on the list refers to, click on it and read the description that appears below before you tick it

7 Click **OK**

8 Click **Delete Files**

UPDATE WINDOWS

Windows is constantly being updated, with additions to its software that can both prevent and fix known problems. You can check to make sure that your computer has all the latest updates and install any new updates.

1 Click [ ], then **Control Panel**

2 Click **System and Security**

3 Click **Windows Update**

4 Click **Check for updates**

5 Windows will search for any updates your computer needs

6 If any updates are found, click **Install updates**

▶ Spring-clean your PC

Install updates automatically

1 Click , then **Control Panel**

2 Click **System and Security**

3 Click **Windows Update**

4 Click **Change settings**

5 Make sure that **Install updates automatically (recommended)** is highlighted

Choose how Windows can install updates

When your computer is online, Windows can automatically check for important updates and install them using these settings. When new updates are available, you can also install them before shutting down the computer.

How does automatic updating help me?

Important updates

Install updates automatically (recommended)

Install new updates: Every day at 03:00

Recommended updates

☑ Give me recommended updates the same way I receive important updates

Who can install updates

☑ Allow all users to install updates on this computer

Microsoft Update

☑ Give me updates for Microsoft products and check for new optional Microsoft software when I update Windows

Software notifications

☐ Show me detailed notifications when new Microsoft software is available

Note: Windows Update might update itself automatically first when checking for other updates. Read our privacy statement online.

6 Click the **down arrows** underneath to select how regularly to install updates (daily is recommended)

7 Make any other changes you wish

8 Click **OK**

CLEAN UP YOUR DESKTOP

When you install a new program, it will usually add an icon – a shortcut to open the program – to your PC's desktop. Your desktop can soon become crowded with icons for programs that you no longer use, so it's good to clean it up.

TIP

For more on finding your way around the desktop, see page 10.

1 Start the Desktop Cleanup Wizard by clicking , then **Control Panel**

2 Click **System and Security**

3 Click **Action Center**

4 Scroll down and click **Troubleshooting** at the bottom of the window

5 Click **Run maintenance tasks**

6 Click **Next** to run the System Maintenance tool, which will clean up unused files and shortcuts, as well as carry out other maintenance tasks

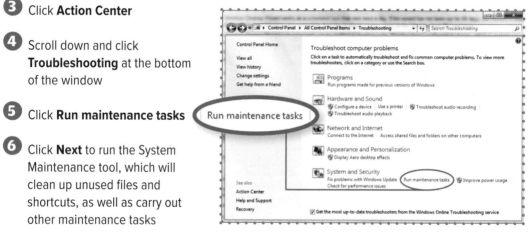

UNINSTALL UNUSED PROGRAMS

Removing unused programs will free up valuable space on your hard drive. For example, you might have installed a Sudoku game or some video-editing software that you no longer use.

1 Click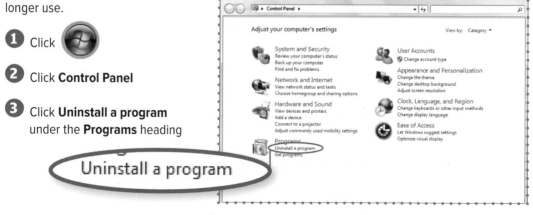

2 Click **Control Panel**

3 Click **Uninstall a program** under the **Programs** heading

▶ Spring-clean your PC

TIP

To uninstall a program you may need to reinsert the disc you used to install it. Keep discs in a safe place.

4 To uninstall a program, click on it and then click **Uninstall** at the top of the list

5 It will be removed straight away so make sure that you're certain you want to delete it

CLEAN OUT A CACHE AND DELETE STORED COOKIES

When you surf the internet, files (known as a cache) are saved onto your computer that hold details about the site you've visited (known as stored cookies). This can be handy and can save you time. For example, when you log into your eBay account, you can tick a box so that it remembers your details and logs you in automatically when you go to the home page.

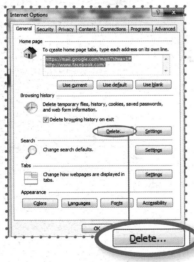

However, by cleaning out your internet cache and deleting stored cookies, you can clear some space on your hard disk, and possibly speed up your broadband connection speed. It also protects your privacy if other people are using your computer.

1 Click **Tools**

2 Click **Internet Options**

3 Click **General** tab

4 Under **Browsing history**, click **Delete**

5 Make sure that **Temporary Internet files** and **Cookies** are ticked

6 Click **Delete**

SECURITY

By reading this chapter you will get to grips with:

- ▶ **Scanning your PC for viruses and spyware**

- ▶ **Protecting yourself online**

▶ Security

SECURE YOUR PC

In order to protect your computer and the data on it you need to have several different types of security software installed on your PC – and keep them all up to date. To protect your computer fully you need to install:

TIP

The Windows 7 operating system has its own firewall and anti-spyware software.

A firewall This is a piece of software that sits between your PC and the internet, protecting your computer from incoming attacks from hackers or malware such as viruses. It's vital that your firewall is switched on.

Anti-virus software This protects against a number of different types of threat, including Trojans and worms. Some anti-virus software will include anti-spyware tools too.

Anti-spyware software This protects your computer from spyware, malicious software that downloads to your computer without your knowledge. Spyware can monitor your activity and collect information about you, and can hijack your browser.

Security software

You can buy a security suite that contains all the elements that you'll need. It may also contain additional features such as a backup program to help you to copy important files or parental control software so that you can manage your child's internet use.

When you install it, security software runs automatically when your PC is on. It scans every file on your machine to spot existing viruses and can take upwards of two hours.

To ensure that you're properly protected:

▶ Download regular security updates. Your chosen program should be set to do this automatically

▶ If you want to use the firewall built into your suite, you'll need to switch off the Windows 7 firewall as you can't run more than one of these at a time

▶ Don't install more than one suite at once as two anti-virus programs or two firewalls can conflict. The exception to this rule is anti-spyware where you can use several programs, though only one of these should be set for automatic scanning

▶ Security suites can place high demands on system resources. If your PC only just meets the requirements of a suite, it's worth looking for an alternative

Free software

Rather than buying a suite, you can download free security programs online. For example, AVG offer a free version of their anti-virus software – go to www.free.avg.com and click **Get basic protection**.

The downside of free programs is that you'll have to download individual programs from different places and you won't get the integrated approach that you'll experience with a bundled suite. You'll have to maintain and monitor each aspect separately (for instance, ensuring that the updates are working) and you're unlikely to get the kind of support you'd receive with a paid-for suite. If you have problems, you may need to search the manufacturer's support pages for assistance.

TIP

You may be offered discounted or free security software when you buy a new computer.

▶ Security

ANTI-VIRUS SOFTWARE EXPLAINED

The best security programs can be set to run largely by themselves, but there are a few things you should know about maintaining your anti-virus software. Here are answers to some of the most common questions.

Does Windows have anti-virus software?

It doesn't have anti-virus software pre-installed, but you can download Microsoft Security Essentials for free, which offers protection against viruses, spyware and other malicious software.

How do I know my anti-virus software is on?

Most anti-virus programs put a flag icon in the notification area of your taskbar (bottom-right of your screen) to show that they're switched on. You can also check your anti-virus setting in the Action Center, found in the System and Security section of the Control Panel (see page 26).

How can I tell if my computer has a virus?

If your computer becomes slow or unresponsive, or if you find that programs that you use all the time are behaving in an unusual way, then your computer may have been infected by a virus.

How many anti-virus programs should I run?

You only need to run one anti-virus program. You should also run a firewall and an anti-spyware program (see pages 202–3).

What's the difference between anti-spyware and anti-virus software?

Anti-virus software protects you against viruses that arrive via email messages or infected files. Anti-spyware programs check for and eliminate other types of malicious software that hide within a program you have chosen to install.

How do I scan for viruses?

Generally, the Scan option should be accessible from the main program page. Check your anti-virus program's settings for a scheduling option so you can set it to run a weekly automated scan.

How often should I update my anti-virus software?

Update your anti-virus program daily. The best anti-virus programs can be set to look for and retrieve updates automatically. In other cases, you may see a message pop up to alert you when updates are available.

CHECKING YOUR SECURITY SETTINGS

You can access the security features of Window 7 through the Action Center.

1 Click

2 Click **Control Panel**

3 Click **System and Security**

4 Click **Action Center**

Solving security issues

If something is wrong, a warning icon will appear in the notification area. For example, if you don't have an anti-virus program installed, you will receive a message here.

1 Click on the flag icon that can be found in the taskbar at the bottom of the screen

2 Click **Open Action Center**

3 From here you can see all security messages in detail and find out what needs attention

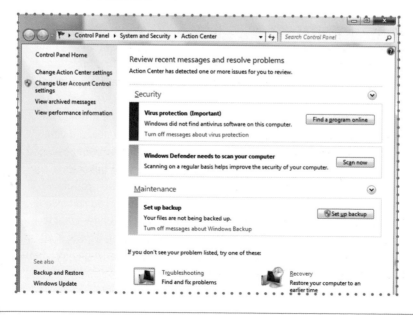

SCAN FOR SPYWARE

If your computer becomes slow or is acting strangely, it could be due to spyware. You can check for spyware using anti-spyware programs such as Microsoft Defender (included with Windows 7).

1 Click

2 Type 'Windows Defender' in the Search box

3 Click on **Windows Defender**

4 Click **Scan now** to scan your computer for spyware. The scan may take a few minutes. You can then ignore, remove or quarantine files

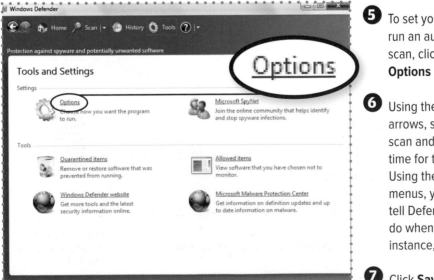

5 To set your computer to run an automatic, daily scan, click **Tools** then **Options**

6 Using the drop-down arrows, select a daily scan and your preferred time for the scan to run. Using the drop-down menus, you can also tell Defender what to do when it finds, for instance, high alert items

7 Click **Save**

TURN ON THE FIREWALL

A firewall protects your computer from incoming attacks from hackers or malware, such as viruses, so it's vital that your firewall is switched on. To turn on the Windows 7 firewall:

1 Click , then **Control panel**

2 Click **System and Security**

3 Click **Windows firewall**

4 Click **Turn Windows firewall on or off** in the sidebar

5 Make sure that there is a tick next to **Turn on Windows Firewall**

6 Click **OK**

TRY THIS

You can also access the Windows firewall by typing 'firewall' in the search box when you click the **Start** button.

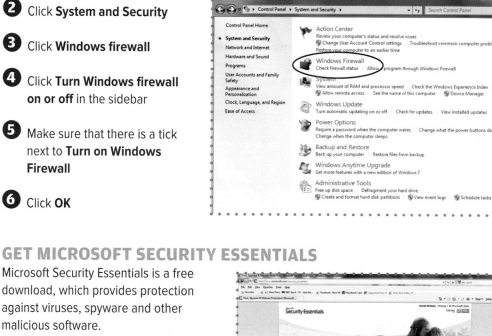

GET MICROSOFT SECURITY ESSENTIALS

Microsoft Security Essentials is a free download, which provides protection against viruses, spyware and other malicious software.

1 Go to **www.microsoft.com/securityessentials**. Click **Download Now**

2 You'll be asked if you want to download the file, click **Run**

3 Wait while the program downloads

4 A 'User Account Control' message may appear. Click **Yes** to continue

5 An installation wizard will help you with the final steps, click **Next**

6 Click **I accept** and then click **Install**

NEXT STEP ⊙

For more on how to stay safe online, see page 204.

security

▶ Security

PC SECURITY TIPS

▶ Security software is only as good as its last update. With new virus and spyware threats constantly emerging, software manufacturers issue regular security updates in response to reported threats. Update your security software at least once a week. Many programs allow you to set it up so that it updates automatically – you can usually find this option under the Settings menu option

▶ When you're downloading free security software, check the name of the product carefully, as some names sound like familiar sources, but are not. Make sure you've downloaded the software from a trusted source. To ensure that you download the right program, type in the full address of the security software's website in the address bar of your browser rather than typing the program's name into a search engine

▶ Don't store passwords or login details on your computer

▶ Don't use a single password for every account you use online

▶ A strong password consists of a mixture of letters (upper and lower case) and numbers

▶ It's crucial to back up your important files regularly (see page 186). Should something happen to your computer, you could lose all of your data. You need to make frequent backup copies of any personal files – photos, videos, emails, for example – but you should also consider making a 'full' backup of your PC's system files and installed applications every so often too

NEXT STEP ▶

For more on backing up your data, see pages 184–9.

INTERNET SECURITY TIPS

Delete your browser history

Your web browser stores a list of the websites you've visited. This means that anyone who uses your computer can view a list of all the websites that you've been to. To delete your Internet Explorer browser history:

1 Click **Tools**

2 Click **Internet options**

3 On the **General** tab under **Browsing history**, select **Delete**

4 Tick **History** in the new window that appears

5 Click **Delete**

Turn off autocomplete

Autocomplete is a function that allows some browsers to 'remember' what you put into online forms. This is useful if you frequently log in to the same sites or are often required to fill in your details in online forms. However, it also means that anyone with access to your computer can see all these details at the click of a button. For shared computers you may wish to turn this off.

1 In **Internet Explorer**, click **Tools**

2 Click **Internet options**

3 Select the **Content** tab

4 Under **Autocomplete** click **Settings**

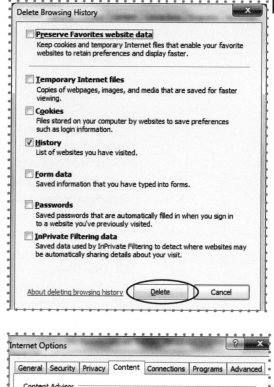

5 Remove the ticks next to **Forms** and **Usernames and passwords on forms**

6 Click **OK**

Block pop-ups

Pop-ups are small windows that open automatically when you visit certain web pages. Many are just annoying or confusing, but they can also contain malicious code or phishing scams.

To block pop-ups in Internet Explorer:

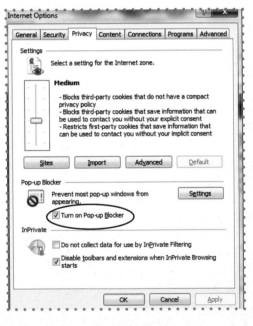

1 Click **Tools**

2 Click **Internet options**

3 Select the **Privacy** tab, and make sure that there's a tick next to **Turn on Pop-up Blocker**

4 You can allow pop-ups from trusted websites. Click on **Settings** and enter your selected web addresses

BE CAREFUL!

Be alert when you're asked to enter personal details such as your credit card details into a web page. A secure web page is prefixed 'https' (the extra 's' stands for secure). You should also check for a padlock icon in your address bar, which denotes a secure web page.

TROUBLE SHOOTING

By reading this chapter you will get to grips with:

▶ **Using Windows Help tools**

▶ **Checking your computer's specifications**

▶ **Restoring your PC**

▶ Troubleshooting

USE WINDOWS HELP

Windows 7 comes with a selection of built-in tools that can help you identify and put right many common computer problems. To access Windows Help:

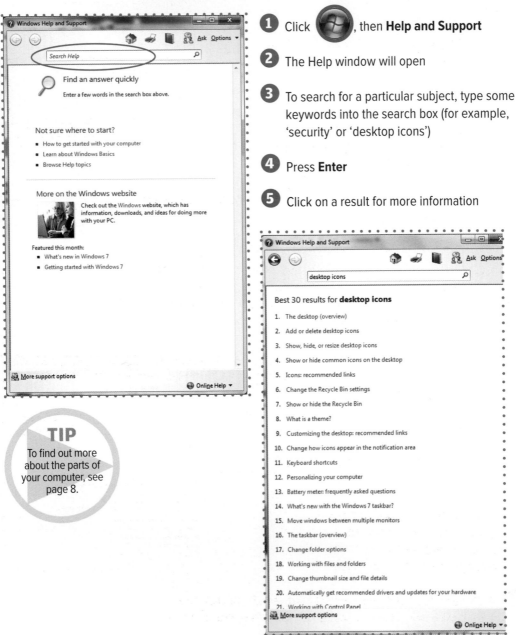

1 Click ⊛, then **Help and Support**

2 The Help window will open

3 To search for a particular subject, type some keywords into the search box (for example, 'security' or 'desktop icons')

4 Press **Enter**

5 Click on a result for more information

TIP
To find out more about the parts of your computer, see page 8.

Include online help in your search results

You can broaden your search by setting the
Help console to include results from online sources.
You'll need to be connected to the internet for this
to work:

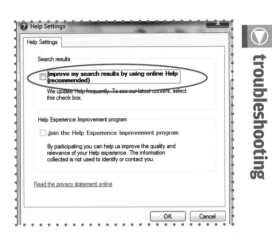

1 Follow Steps 1 and 2 opposite and then click
Options on the toolbar

2 Click **Settings**

3 In the box make sure there's a tick next to
**Improve my search results by using Online
Help (recommended)**

4 Click **OK**. Up-to-date online results will now be included in any future
searches you carry out

CHECK YOUR COMPUTER'S SPECIFICATIONS

Before you can find out what's wrong with your computer, you may need
more information about your computer. To find out your computer's
specifications – for example, the type of processor it has and how much
memory is installed – follow these steps:

1 Click , then **Control Panel**

2 Click **System and Security**

3 Click **System**

4 This brings up a box showing basic
information about your computer

5 To get further information on your
graphics card, sound card and
attached peripherals, click **Device
Manager** on the left-hand menu

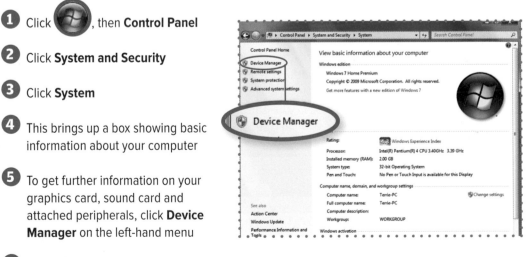

6 You'll see a list of different types of hardware. Right click on a
device you'd like to know more about. Select **Properties** to see
more details

▶ Troubleshooting

GET HELP ONLINE

If you know that your problem lies with a specific program, such as photo-editing software, or a device, such as your DVD drive, then your first port of call should be the manufacturer's website. Once you're on the site, have a look for a link that says **Support** or **Help**. Click it and check out the frequently asked questions (FAQs) section, where you'll find common problems and solutions.

On some websites, you can also post a message in an online forum asking for help, send the support team an email or have a one-to-one online chat with a technician.

Error messages

If your computer is showing an error message, make a precise note of what it says or use your cursor to highlight the message and press **Ctrl+C** to copy it. Next, enter the error message into a search engine such as www.google.co.uk or www.yahoo.co.uk (type it in, or press **Ctrl+V** to paste it straight in), and press search.

If you can't find anything useful in the results that come up, have a go at typing a brief description of your problem and then running a new search. And, if at first you don't succeed, reword your problem and try again.

Using forums

If you can't find a solution with a general internet search, try searching the list of useful websites and forums opposite. If the sites listed don't provide the answer to your specific problem, you can post your question in one of the forums. Include the full details of your problem, including error messages and any relevant make and model information, and state which operating system you're using. Bear in mind that the respondents aren't necessarily qualified computer experts.

Useful websites and forums

www.annoyances.org
Collection of advice that's great for solving Windows-related problems

www.askdavetaylor.com
Expert advice on a wide variety of technical topics

www.bleepingcomputer.com
Online community that has tutorials, forums and tips

www.compukiss.com
'Keeping It Short and Simple', this site is great for tips

www.computerhope.com
A support site with good forums

www.computing.net
Offers useful, active forums

www.geekstogo.com
Forums that allow you to take advantage of helpful technicians

www.helpwithpcs.com
Useful tips and explanations, as well as free tutorials

www.supportfreaks.com
Use the 'Freebies' service to get support

http://support.microsoft.com
Microsoft's official support site for those using Windows PCs

www.which.co.uk
Lots of computing and security help and advice. To contact the Which? Computing Helpdesk service, you'll need to have to hand the following code: WIN7COMP311.

► Troubleshooting

RESTORE YOUR PC

If you're unable to fix your computer yourself, you can use a feature called System Restore. It works by automatically (and frequently) taking a snapshot of your system settings. It's then possible to restore your PC back to one of these points if something goes wrong.

1 Click , then **Control Panel**

2 Click **All Programs**

3 Click **Accessories**

4 Click **System tools**

5 Click **System Restore**

6 Click **Next**

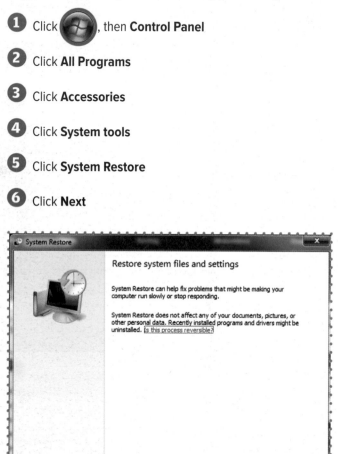

7 Select the restore point you want to use by clicking on it

8 Click **Next**

9 Click **Finish**. Your computer will shut down and restart

RESOURCES

▶ Jargon Buster

3G The third generation of mobile networks, which allows large amounts of data to be sent wirelessly. Mobile broadband operates over the 3G network.

ADSL (Asymmetric digital subscriber line) A way of sending data over a copper wire telephone line.

Adware Software that tracks your web use to determine your interests and deliver relevant ads.

Anti-spyware Software that prevents and/or removes spyware.

Anti-virus Software that scans for viruses and removes them from your computer.

Application A type of program that's used by a person, as opposed to a program that's used by a computer.

Backup A copy of your files or programs for safekeeping.

Blog A regularly updated online journal.

Blu-ray A high-definition DVD format developed by Sony. A Blu-ray disc can hold nine hours of high-definition (HD) video and around 23 hours of standard-definition (SD) video on a 50GB disc.

Browser (or web browser) The software that enables you to view web pages. Often these contain phishing filters.

Cursor A cursor is the symbol onscreen that shows where the next character will appear; the cursor may also be shown as an arrow called a pointer.

Desktop The main screen you see when you start your computer. From here you can save files and access programs.

Download To transfer data from a remote computer to your own computer over the internet.

Driver Software that allows your computer to communicate with devices such as a printer.

Email client A computer program that manages emails. Emails are stored on your computer, and you only need to be connected to the internet to send and receive emails.

Ethernet A means of connecting computers together using cables.

Firewall Software (or hardware) that blocks unwanted communication from, and often to, the internet.

Firewire A type of connection that is fast and well suited to transferring large amounts of data, such as video footage, from devices.

Forum An online message board.

Gigabytes (GB) A measurement of data storage. Eight bits make up a byte; 1,024 bytes make a kilobyte; 1,024 kilobytes make a megabyte; 1,024 megabytes make a gigabyte.

Hard disk The main long-term storage space used by your computer to store data. Also known as a hard drive.

Icon A small picture that represents an object or program.

ISP (Internet Service Provider) An ISP is the company that enables and services your connection to the internet.

Jpeg A file format that refers to a compressed image.

Keywords Significant, descriptive words used as search terms.

Malware Malicious software. A generic term for any program that is harmful to your computer, for example, a virus.

Mbps (Megabits per second) A measure of the speed of data transfer, often used when talking about the speed of broadband.

⏵ Jargon Buster

Megabyte (Mb) A measurement of data storage. Eight bits make up a byte; 1,024 bytes make a kilobyte; 1,024 kilobytes make a megabyte; 1,024 megabytes make a gigabyte.

Megahertz (MHz) The speed of your computer's processor (its brain) is measured in megahertz. One MHz is one million cycles per second.

Memory stick Small, portable device used to store and transfer data. It plugs into a USB port and is also called a USB, flash drive or pen drive.

Microfilter A device that attaches to your telephone socket and enables you to make voice calls and use broadband at the same time via ADSL.

Modem A device that allows a computer to send information over a telephone line.

MP3 player A portable music player that plays digital music.

Network A system of communication between two or more computers.

Operating System The software that manages your computer.

PDF Portable Document Format, a file format created by Adobe that allows pages of text and graphics to be viewed on any computer.

Phishing A type of email scam where you're tricked into giving away personal details by being directed to a spoof website that resembles the site of an official organisation (a bank, for example).

Plug-in A small program that adds extra features to your web browser.

Podcast A type of online radio (or video) show that you can subscribe to. Files are downloaded and listened to offline.

Pop-up A small window that appears over an item (word or picture) on your computer screen to give additional information.

Port A computer socket into which you plug equipment.

Processor The main brain of your computer.

RAM Your computer's short-term memory.

Ripping Copying data from a CD or DVD to a computer.

Router A device that routes data between computers and other devices. Routers can connect computers to each other or connect a computer to the internet.

Screensaver The image or set of images that appear when your computer is idle for a certain period of time.

Security suite A bundle of security programs to protect your PC.

Social networking A way for people to socialise online, typically via a website, such as Facebook or MySpace.

Software A general term for programs used to operate computers and related devices.

Soundcard This is an internal part of your computer and is responsible for outputting sound.

Spam Unsolicited junk email.

Spam filter Software or a system that helps to filter spam from your inbox.

Spreadsheet A spreadsheet is a collection of data arranged in rows and columns. A spreadsheet program lets you manage these electronically.

Spyware Software that secretly installs on your computer and is able to track your internet behaviour and send details to a third party.

Tagging Process of adding descriptive keywords to a piece of information, such as a photo or web page, to aid in the search for it.

▶ Jargon Buster

Terabyte See megabyte: 1,024 gigabytes make a terabyte.

Trojan A computer virus that disguises itself as an innocent program to entice people to install it. Trojans can allow third parties complete access to your computer remotely.

Upload Process of sending files from your computer to the internet.

USB (Universal Serial Bus) A connection technology that allows you to easily transfer data. *See also* Memory stick

Virus A malevolent program that spreads from computer to computer within another program or file.

Voice over Internet Protocol (VoIP) Term used to describe making phone calls over the internet rather than via a standard phone network.

Web browser *See* Browser

Webcam A video camera attached to or integrated into your computer.

Webmail Email accounts accessed through your web browser.

Worm Similar to a virus, except a worm doesn't need to attach itself to a document and can spread via the internet.

⏵ Index

index

▶ Index

index

ABOUT THE CONSULTANT EDITOR TERRIE CHILVERS
Terrie Chilvers is a freelance writer and journalist specialising in computing, technology and games. She lives in London and contributes to *Which? Computing* magazine.

▶ Further help

HAVING PROBLEMS
WITH YOUR COMPUTER?

A few years ago **Which? Computing** launched an online Helpdesk service.
The team has a combined experience of over forty years and promises
to answer questions within two working days.

To date, the team has answered tens of thousands of queries from readers,
and there's no PC problem they won't tackle.

As a reader of **Computing Made Easy for the Over 50s**,
you can now access this indispensable service absolutely free.

To submit a question for the Helpdesk*, simply go to
www.which.co.uk/computinghelpdesk

Enter your query and, where it asks for a membership number,
simply enter the code that you'll find on the page of 'Useful
websites and forums' in the Troubleshooting chapter.

*This service is only available online